BETTER RECOVERY FROM VIRAL ILLNESSES

DR DARREL HO-YEN

**BMSc(Hons), MBChB,
FRCPath, FRCP, MD, DSc**

D1439885

DODONA BOOKS

FIRST EDITION: 1985
SECOND EDITION: 1987
THIRD EDITION: 1993, Reprinted 1994
FOURTH EDITION: 1999, Reprinted 2003
FIFTH EDITION: 2008

ISBN 0-9511090-7-3

Published and distributed by:

DODONA BOOKS
"Corriemuir", Viewhill
Culloden Moor
Inverness, IV2 5EA

(www.dodonabooks.co.uk)

British Library Cataloging in Publication Data
A catalogue record of this book is available from the British Library.

CONTENTS

ABOUT THE AUTHOR

Dr Darrel Ho-Yen was born in Guyana, South America, but finished his schooling in London. After a year's Voluntary Services Overseas in the Caribbean, he studied at Dundee University medical school. He completed his training at the Regional Virus Laboratory, Glasgow. He is now Head of Microbiology at Raigmore Hospital, Inverness, Director of the Scottish Toxoplasma Reference Laboratory and Lyme Borreliosis testing laboratory, and Honorary Clinical Senior Lecturer at Aberdeen University.

Dr Ho-Yen has had extensive experience in managing patients with Post Viral Fatigue Syndrome and the first edition of this book (1985) was the first book on the subject. His other books are: co-author of **"Diseases of Infection"** (1987,1993) and co-editor of **"Human Toxoplasmosis"** (1992), both published by Oxford University Press; co-author of **"Ticks"**, Mercat Press (1998, 2006); and section editor of **"Science of Laboratory Diagnosis"**, ISIS Medical (1998), John Wiley (2005).

His experience of the needs of patients with chronic illnesses prompted him to write **"Unwind! Understand and control life, be better!!"** (combines relaxation with stress management techniques) in 1991 (reprinted 1994) and **"Climbing Out of the Pit of Life"** (deals with recovering from great loss) in 1995. Dr Ho-Yen has published numerous scientific papers and lectures extensively.

PREFACE

The first edition of this book was printed in April 1985, and was the first book in the world on Post Viral Fatigue Syndrome/Myalgic Encephalomyelitis (PVFS/ME). Since then there have been some 60 books. Many of these books are highly scientific and have many references. However, many patients do not want such precise information, but instead they want more details about how to deal with their illness. In this book, **I have concentrated on what I tell patients when I see them.** The cost of this book has reflected greater costs. The previous edition was offered on the internet for £206.71. **Nevertheless, I had found that patients needed much support and that hours could be spent on the telephone (at great cost) or the greater costs of consultations.**

Many patients have commented on what they have found to be most helpful. Over the years, I have spoken to very many groups of patients throughout Britain. At these talks, many have felt that my pictorial slides were very useful. **Thus, in this edition I have included many of the slides that I use to illustrate my talks.**

This book is designed to be read by ill patients with very poor concentration. The language, type-setting and repetition are necessary. Some healthy individuals may find this style annoying, but I hope that they will understand. **Again and again, patients have asked for a book which motivates and sets out a precise plan for recovery.** These have been the main objectives of this book.

No book is published by the efforts of only one person. **Rob Polson** has been exceptionally helpful in getting me scientific papers and proof-reading the many drafts. I have been grateful for help with illustrations from **Alan McGinley, Audrey Grant** and **Seonaid McLaren. Nicola Ho-Yen** has been very helpful, and my sons **Gregory and Colan** have been very supportive. **Dr David Ashburn** has been superb in preparing this manuscript for the printers; he has managed to meet every deadline and overcome all obstacles. **David Ritchie and Lynne Mackay** of A4 Design and Print Ltd have been extremely cooperative and very easy to work with. Lastly, I am indebted to **Barbara Reed** who has provided me with outstanding secretarial support; she has shown great patience and understanding through many drafts of this book.

Darrel Ho-Yen
2008

CHAPTER ONE
WHY BUY THIS BOOK?

This book is expensive compared to similar books. So, why should you buy this book? The reasons are in this chapter but this book is not for everyone. A lot depends on what sort of person you are and how you respond to illness.

This was the first book in the world published on this illness in 1985. It is the only book that is in its fifth edition. **This tells you that it documented the problem before anyone else, and it has changed with advances in knowledge** more than others. Yet this book has great disadvantages. The solution it proposes is difficult as the principal player is yourself. **This book demands a lot of you.** If you are afraid of this commitment, read no further as this book is not for you.

We buy books that we like. This is fine if reading is for enjoyment, but if it is for knowledge our likes are less important. **If the object is better health, again, it is not about one's likes.** Most patients find this book hard reading, many dislike the demands being made on them. Indeed, 20% of patients cannot cope with these demands and decide it is too much to ask of a sick person. Thus, **you need to choose this book because it can make you better rather than because you like it.** The decision to make any choice or purchase is dependant on several factors. Here, the most important are: the other options, what a book offers and what suits you best.

OTHER OPTIONS

In today's world of the Internet we are all faced with many options. Indeed we probably have too many choices. How does one make a good decision? One answer may lie in our understanding of how we make these choices.

1. Cheap advice
For most patients, this is easily available. Friends and relatives are quick to bring to your attention newspaper articles, radio and television programmes. In addition, the Internet has websites that offer advice and ways to get better. With so much information, patients have difficult choices, especially as their minds are not functioning normally. One consideration is the cost. When things are free or cheap, it is often because they cannot be sold. What they offer is often less than what is required. **This book provides a complete strategy for recovery.**

2. Presentation
When my sons were young, they liked large and heavy presents. They felt that these would have the best content. So, one Christmas, I put their presents in a

large box and added a big rock. They really looked forward to opening their presents. And they would have thrown the rocks at me, but they were too heavy. **Many treatments are well presented with the offer of quick, guaranteed results.** For an ill person, such alternative remedies to traditional medicine are very attractive. The desire to be better and back to normal is so strong that it seems reasonable "to try anything". Sadly, there are many such treatments, often with the testimonial of someone who has benefited. Like diets, there are many and varied, but few that work for most individuals. Patients must separate presentation from substance. **You need to judge if a treatment can deliver on the promise of getting better.**

3. Good value

Good value is not the same for everyone. Some like quantity, others like quality. However, for an ill patient it is about getting better. This book is 3-5 times more expensive than others. Yet, it is **10 times cheaper than a consultation.** The last edition was offered for sale on the Internet for more than £206.71, a special "low price" of £89.75 and ex-library copies at a "low price" of £67.00. **Why are people prepared to spend these sums on a book?** Over the years, and four editions of this book, the key messages on energy have not changed; but the other aspects of the book have changed for emphasis, effect or what works. **This book is good value as it represents what I say to patients when I see them.** I had found that often I was repeating myself and hence this book is what I would say to you in a consultation.

THIS BOOK

It is important that you are clear of what this book offers. Over two decades, each edition has been changed to reflect what has helped patients to get better.

1. The Strategy
Most books and advice from charities have adopted aspects of my management strategy as described in the first edition published in 1985. It is nice that so many others have wanted to copy my advice!! **However, only this book has the whole management strategy.** There are problems when you use substitutes. It is like a meal of beef stew; if you substitute yoghurt for the cream and soya protein for the beef, it will just not be the same. **This book focuses on helping you to stay within your energy limits so that your body can use its energy to recover.** There are separate chapters on gaining energy, making energy last and how to stop losing energy. The strategy is based on what has worked or failed with patients.

2. Being selfish
Before they became unwell, most patients were generous, loving individuals. They were keen to help others and did much good. However, I believe that these attitudes are inappropriate for someone who is ill. **When you are ill, you need to focus on getting better, to be selfish.** Many patients find such statements abhorrent. They still want to be the hero. Perhaps, before you can truly help others, you must be able to help yourself. In consultation, I would spend most time in conveying this hard message to patients.

3. Monitoring progress

If patients follow my strategy, they improve 10% every two months. The very best patients can improve 20% every two months. **This means that most patients get better in 10-12 months.** There is no quick recovery, but slow gradual progress as patients change their lifestyle. However, how do you monitor progress? I believe in a daily diary, taking only 2-3 minutes per day. Patients hate the daily diary, but if you cannot do a daily diary, I do not see you. The diary is like a compass, it ensures you keep making progress. **It is the best way to understand how your behaviour influences progress.** Two people can stay in bed all day, but one will get better and the other will get worse. The diary will tell you why. As with many things, what you hate can help.

4. Motivation

Many readers have said that this is the most important aspect of the book. Patients and their carers are often given advice, but the philosophy and reasoning behind the advice is not available. This book aims at providing knowledge to reinforce the management strategy. **The entire management of patients is based on what has worked on other patients.** Thus, you are reassured that others have faced similar problems and have overcome them. Overall, 80% of patients who are able to adopt the philosophy in the book have got better.

As with all motivation, there has to be reinforcement of key messages. **This book is designed to be read by ill patients.** The layout is easy to read and repetition takes into account poor memory and concentration. Thus, a few pages can be read at a time. It is also recommended that this book is read again and again to reinforce key messages. **It is a great help if the patient and carer can read the book together.** The excellent track record of this strategy and its durability is a testimony of the many patients who have been helped.

YOUR BEST CHOICE

What is one person's best choice may not suit someone else. This individuality depends on several factors:

1. Your role
Some patients like to help themselves and for these, this book is ideal. However, other patients may feel that it is the doctor's responsibility to help them; and for these individuals, this book is not for you. **About 20% of patients find this book too demanding** and do not like the approach. Others feel that they are too ill to undertake the responsibility of getting better. A lot also depends on the carer. I insist on seeing husband and wives together as it is important that both get the same message. It is a great burden for a patient to have to explain what was said to a partner. The feelings of the carer are also important in deciding if the patient should follow this book. A joint decision produces best results.

2. Crusades
Two decades ago, patients had difficulties in getting a diagnosis. Treatment was "nothing can be done" or "the disease will burn itself out". To get a diagnosis and correct treatment required a crusade. Now, diagnosis should not be a problem. **However, management is still variable.** Many patients are involved in a crusade to get appropriate treatment. This takes much energy, and I believe that this energy is best spent on getting better. If

14

your crusade is to the detriment of your getting better, this book is not for you.

3. Commitment
This book is for those who can commit to getting themselves better. **If you have this commitment, this book is for you.** If you want to understand the illness and its effects on you, this book will give you the information. You must make getting better your main objective. If you feel responsible for others and have other things that you "must do", do not buy this book. This book teaches about the use of energy by using the analogy of energy as money. **If you are good with money it will be easy to learn the use of energy.** This book requires great commitment as getting better is a big task.

SUMMARY

How long have you been ill? What have you tried? How successful has it been? These questions require answers. The answers determine if you should buy this book. If you are prepared to follow all that is in this book, you will get better in 10-12 months. This book requires an understanding of the illness, energy and yourself. **You will have to change many things that you are doing as they are not helping you to recover.** This book does not offer quick, easy solutions. However, if a change of lifestyle returns you to good health, is it not worth the sacrifice?

CHAPTER TWO
THE PROBLEM

Many feel that they should be able to avoid all infections. This is wrong. **Infections are a necessary stimulus to the immune system.** Unfortunately there are many, including medical practitioners, who are happy to go jogging to stimulate their cardiovascular system but who moan when they get influenza. An influenza infection is the best test of immune function – it is the marathon race for the body's immune system.

When people become ill, they expect to recover quickly. **Yet, it is common to hear: "I have never been well since my flu two years ago".** The truth is that many patients do not return to good health after infections. For these patients, months or years after the acute illness, there is excessive tiredness and poor recovery after minor exercise. Worse, other complaints develop such as dizziness, poor vision, joint pains, muscle aches and twitches. Why does this happen? What is the illness called? What should these patients do?

NAMES

The illness has been described as the disease with a thousand names. Historically, in America, **epidemic neuromyasthenia** was used. In Europe, **Iceland disease** described an outbreak in Iceland during 1948-1949; and **Royal Free disease** an outbreak in that London hospital during 1955-1958. Subsequently, **myalgic encephalomyelitis** (ME) has been the name used, but not all patients have muscle pain ("myalgia"). In America, **Chronic Fatigue Syndrome** (CFS) has been advocated. However, the definition of this Syndrome requires the active exclusion of some 50 conditions; it is a more useful research definition than one for everyday use. I like **Post Viral Fatigue Syndrome (PVFS)** as most patients have a viral-like infection on the onset. It does not mean that viruses cause the illness. Indeed it is known that other infections (such as toxoplasma or Lyme borreliosis) can produce a similar illness. **'Viral' refers to the fact that most patients have a viral-like illness (with fever and malaise) at the onset.**

CASE HISTORIES

Mr A was very athletic and previously healthy. He played squash to a high standard and was a scratch golf player. At 31 years of age he was very fit and accustomed to playing 3 games of squash, 3 games of 18 holes of golf and doing the gardening, all in the same weekend. Then one New Year, after a walk in the hills, he developed a flu-like illness. After two days he felt better and returned to work. However, he continued to feel tired. His squash deteriorated from having lost only one match prior to the New Year, to it being unusual for him to win a match. **Lack of stamina was the main problem as he usually won the first game but would then lose the next two.** His golf was similar with a good first nine holes but a disastrous last nine. At the end of the game he was hardly able to lift the golf club. Two years after the illness started he gave up squash altogether. A year later he stopped playing golf. He took early retirement 12 years after the start of his illness.

Although women and men have an equal chance of developing the illness, it appears that women are more likely to become chronic sufferers. The reasons for this are unknown. Some have suggested that the preponderance of women suggests that PVFS is a hysterical illness. However, the almost equal numbers of men and women affected at the onset of the disease argues against such an interpretation.

Mrs B was a 30 year-old, energetic, social worker who skied and was a good squash player. She developed a "3-day flu" in January one year. After this she never felt well. In the first few months after the illness started, her principal complaint was excessive tiredness. She needed to sleep a lot and could feel tired even after a good night's sleep. **Over the first year, she stopped playing sport and her social life was considerably reduced as she was always tired in the evening.** But the worst was not yet over. In the second year, she developed a rhinitis which resulted in her nose being blocked all day and running all night. Despite numerous tablets and a sinus wash-out, there was no improvement, but instead her nasal secretions produced a cough and breathlessness at night. Later that year, she was admitted to hospital with asthma. By the end of the year, it was felt that she was allergic to dairy products, and she had had further surgery to her nose. After nine years, she still feels exhausted and her nose still runs.

All ages can be affected by PVFS (Figure 1). Master C was a 9 year-old boy who experienced severe tiredness after a flu-like illness. Over the next year he was an intermittent attender at school and was suspected of having school phobia. However, the educational psychologist felt that the boy had an organic illness and a detailed examination of his history showed that he had previously enjoyed school and its activities. With proper management, he slowly returned to good health. **The outlook is much better in younger people, but all ages can show dramatic improvement.**

Whereas most patients become very frustrated with their illness after a few months, the length of illness can be very long. Mrs D has had pain and fatigue on walking for 15 years. This is in addition to other symptoms which have meant that she has consulted many doctors in many hospitals. **Mr E** has not been well for 29 years. Apart from being easily tired, he remembers a marked inability to concentrate after the start of the original illness. Over the years as he has got older, **with each minor illness he seemed to develop some more symptoms.** However, there is some consolation that his tiredness is less worrying now that he is retired than when he was forty.

Common to almost all patients is tiredness and exhaustion after minimal exercise. In most, this produces a need for rest and sleep often accompanied by the frustration of: "All I can do is sleep". **Yet, some**

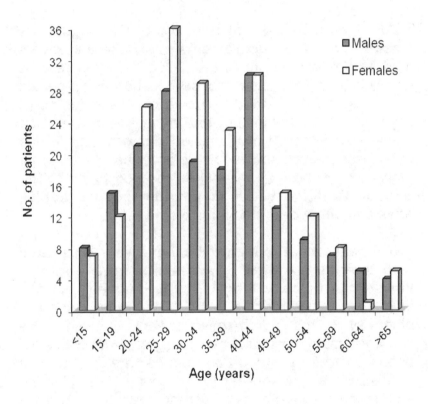

Figure 1 Age distribution of patients
All ages are affected. There is a double peak at 25-29 years
and 40-44 years in both sexes. In this study the sex incidence
was almost equal (204 : 177 = 1.2F : 1.0M)[1].

patients such as Miss F are unable to sleep properly. She is excessively tired, goes to bed and sleeps for 3-4 hours, but then awakes. She then spends the rest of the night tossing and turning. Her mind wanders, her muscles twitch and move on their own accord. She gets up, goes to the toilet, has a cup of tea, but still is unable to sleep on returning to bed. Similarly, rest is not easy for **Mrs G who gets intense pain and burning in her muscles after exertion.** The pain is so intense that she needs strong analgesics. She cries herself to sleep when the pain is particularly bad.

Although fatigue can be a very worrying symptom, at least it is a normal sensation and experienced by everyone. **Some of the more unusual symptoms that can occur after viral infections are much more disturbing. Miss H** suffered from shooting pains at the top of her head and in her spine several times a day. **Miss I** has periods when she is unable to say what she is thinking, and when she can speak, she may forget huge parts of the previous conversation. **Miss J** suffered from dizziness which is made worse by travelling in a car or on a bus. Even a short journey results in her being totally disorientated and lost, so she walks everywhere.

For many patients, the family is the most important unit. The family, with its other members being normal and healthy, is able to offer physical help and moral support. A common statement is : "If it were not for the family, I would have given up a long time ago". Fortunately, PVFS does not usually affect the whole family. **Yet, for Mr and Mrs K, they have the unusual distinction of both being affected.** Worse still, their 14 year-old son also has PVFS. At the moment, this just appears to be a particularly unlucky combination of circumstances. **Whole families are only rarely affected, although it is not uncommon to have more than one member of the family with PVFS.**

SUMMARY

1. Before the illness, many patients were athletic, very productive individuals with good health.

2. Women and men have equal chances of developing the illness, but women may be more likely to become chronic sufferers.

3. All ages are affected, but the outlook is much better in young people.

4. Post Viral Fatigue Syndrome may be the best name for the illness. Other common names are myalgic encephalomyelitis and Chronic Fatigue Syndrome.

Important facts

It is not uncommon for people to develop severe fatigue after a viral-like illness. The illness may last months, years or decades if it is not managed correctly.

CHAPTER THREE
HISTORY

The history of this book reflects how PVFS (ME, CFS) is perceived by the public and the medical profession. This is not surprising as when it was first published in 1985 it was designed to offer help to patients and doctors. **Over the last two decades, there have been major changes in the book.** The first edition had a chapter on herpes simplex, hepatitis and AIDS as these infections can cause fatigue. In the next edition, this chapter was replaced by chapters on self-help groups, alternative medicine and employment. This edition has a new chapter on Lyme borreliosis and PVFS. The book has always responded to the comments being made by the users. **The emphasis is based on what patients and doctors have found useful.**

All editions contained chapters on: clinical symptoms, psychological problems, food allergies and the role of exercise. **The need for a daily diary** and its importance in relation to exercise has always been emphasised. **The key role of energy** meant that the fourth edition had three chapters on this subject compared to one in the third edition. The fourth edition also had a chapter on young people to reflect their peculiar problems and their management. **All editions have been influenced by readers** asking for change or no change, for example many have liked the figures and have requested that they should be kept in future editions.

INFECTIONS

Everyone has an average 2-7 viral infections every year and these diseases cause over half of the absenteeism from work. The vast majority of people recover from infections within a couple of days, or at the most some weeks (Figure 2). **In the few who do not recover, and who develop PVFS,** the outlook can be bleak. Illness can continue over years, or even decades, and a wide spectrum of complaints can occur. **Many patients become depressed and contemplation of suicide is not uncommon.**

Recent medical research shows that PVFS does exist. **The suggestion that this illness is "all in the mind" is just not acceptable.** Over the last years, there has been a massive increase in knowledge of this illness. Some of the recent discoveries have been due to the application of modern technology, others have been a result of workers in different areas of medicine applying their expertise to PVFS. **One can say unequivocally that there is no reason to doubt the truth of many complaints in PVFS patients.**

Most people are aware that infections may occur in outbreaks (large numbers become affected) but most

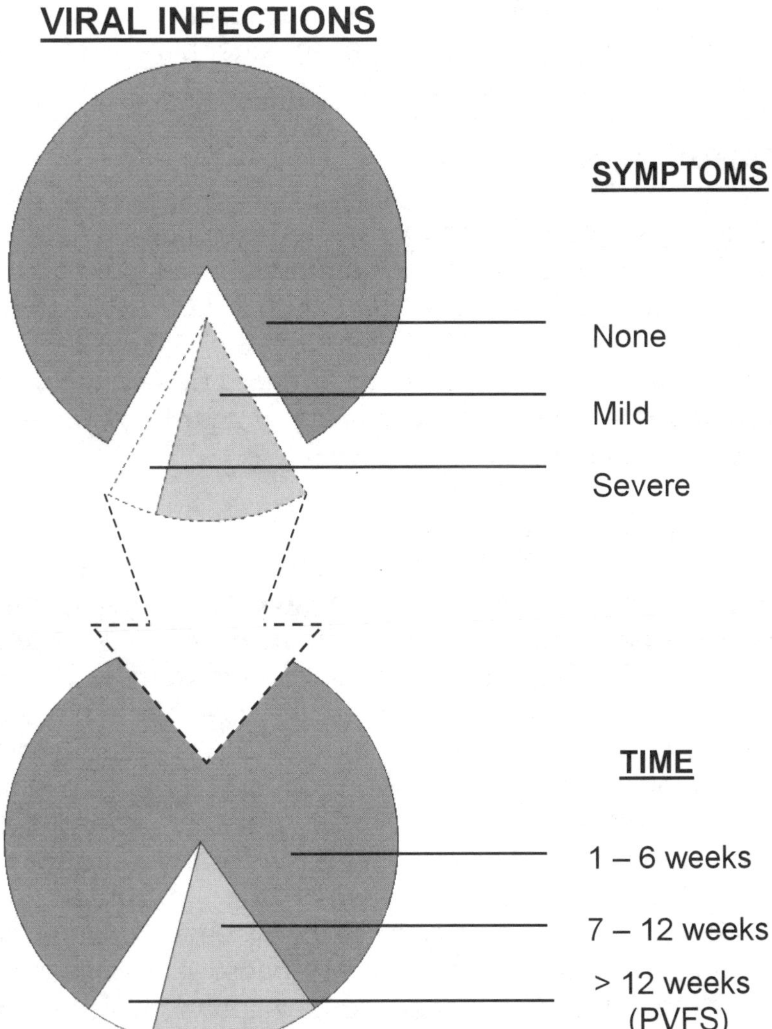

VIRAL INFECTIONS

SYMPTOMS

None

Mild

Severe

TIME

1 – 6 weeks

7 – 12 weeks

> 12 weeks
(PVFS)

Figure 2 Viral infections and recovery
All of the population have viral infections, and most produce
minor or no symptoms. In those with symptoms, recovery in
the majority occurs in 1-6 weeks. A few patients take more
than 12 weeks to recover and develop PVFS.

infections cause problems by sporadic cases (one or two become affected). PVFS has a long history of both outbreaks and sporadic cases.

OUTBREAKS

Outbreaks have been reported worldwide. Most outbreaks have been in temperate countries but tropical areas have also been affected. I do not believe that the earliest outbreak of PVFS was in 1934. **I believe that PVFS has existed for as long as there have been viral infections – from the very start of man's existence.** Important examples are as follows:

1. Encephalitis lethargica.
What is this? Why is it not heard of now? These are good questions. **Even to the layman, lethargy and sleepiness coupled with disease of the brain (encephalitis lethargica) has some similarity to PVFS.** In addition, there is evidence that the disease occurred in all age groups, but chiefly in the 20-30 age group; social status and occupation played no part in determining those affected[2]. Encephalitis lethargica is probably an early description of severe PVFS. **An early account of encephalitis lethargica was the outbreak in Copenhagen, 1657.** Cases of the disease appeared to be related to epidemics of fevers, most likely influenza. After the 1918-1919 pandemic of influenza which killed 30 million people worldwide, a large outbreak of encephalitis lethargica followed. One reason for this is that the influenza strain of 1918-1919 was neuropathogenic (i.e. particularly likely to attack the nervous system). When there was widespread vaccination with a similar influenza vaccine in the United

States in 1976, there were many cases of Guillain-Barré Syndrome (a nervous illness causing paralysis) complicating vaccination. **There have been no large outbreaks of a neuropathogenic influenza since 1918-1919,** and coincidentally there have been no outbreaks of encephalitis lethargica. **Nevertheless, the medical descriptions of encephalitis lethargica encompass the full spectrum of PVFS/ME.**

2. Arboviral encephalitis.

Many arboviruses (viruses that are arthropod-borne i.e. insect transmitted) produce encephalitis. Well-documented complications are fatigue, weakness, drowsiness, inability to concentrate and nervousness. **Some were described as "convalescent-fatigue syndrome".** One epidemic of St Louis encephalitis in 1933 not only shows many similarities to PVFS, but also is instructive on the aftermath of an epidemic. When asked: "Has health been the same, better or worse since the attack of encephalitis?" Responses showed 42% to be the same, 34% to be worse and 24% to be better[3]. **It is perhaps quite revealing to PVFS patients to know that 24% of people can feel better after the illness.**

Other interesting findings of this outbreak were that mainly adults were involved, and many were incapable of working. Two-thirds of the patients studied were restored to good health with **only 7% having total disability.** This figure is probably a reasonable indication of the prognosis in PVFS.

SPORADIC CASES

One problem with an emphasis on outbreaks is that **it can be forgotten that most cases occur in ones and twos and are the more common presentation of PVFS.** At any one time, there may be 10-20 different viruses circulating in the community, and any may rarely produce PVFS. As these viruses can be difficult to identify, diagnosis is often made on the clinical picture. **There is a temptation for patients to blame their doctor for not having the wit to request the correct test.** If there is to be any blame, it is that current tests are not adequate to answer the questions being asked. **A detailed study in the north of Scotland has shown that doctors found PVFS in 1.3 per 1000 of their patients (Figure 3)[4].** In this study, 71% of doctors accepted the existence of PVFS. This is a high acceptance rate for Britain, but it means that the figure of 1.3/1000 of the population is probably an under-estimate.

PATIENT GROUPS

Groups of patients that develop PVFS are: (occupation only known in 91% of cases)[4].

Teachers and students	22%
Retired	16%
Housewives	13%
Service industries	11%
Secretarial/clerical staff	9%
Unskilled workers	8%
Hospital workers	7%
Professional workers	5%

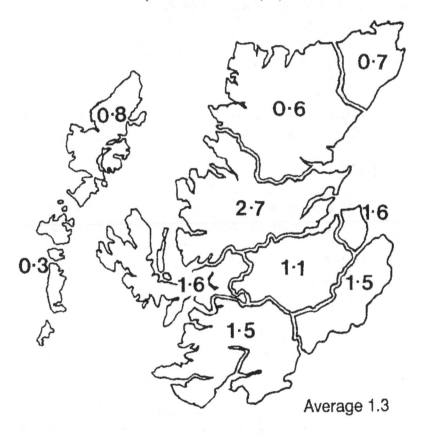

PREVALENCE OF PVFS
(Patients / 1000 population)

0·7
0·6
0·8
2·7
1·6
0·3
1·1
1·6
1·5
1·6
1·5

Average 1.3

Figure 3 Prevalence of PVFS in North Scotland
There is more illness in areas of greater population. The prevalence varies between 0.3 to 2.7 per 1000 of the population. For the whole area, 1.3/1000 of the population were affected[4].

Most patient are in groups most exposed to infection. Among the unskilled workers, some were illiterate and so could not be influenced by magazine articles. Teachers and students have an environment rich in viruses. Children bring infections home and this may explain high levels among housewives. Interestingly, hospital workers are a small group.

Many patients feeling unwell years after a viral infection are not routinely managed by specialist services. Help for these patients lies in their own ability to understand their illness and to adopt attitudes that change their lifestyle. This book provides such a plan.

SUMMARY

1. The 5 editions of this book document the history of changing management in PVFS over 2 decades.

2. Outbreaks of PVFS divert attention from the importance that all viruses may rarely cause PVFS and that most cases are sporadic.

3. The full history of PVFS is unknown. Encephalitis lethargica and arboviral encephalitis are good candidates for early descriptions of PVFS.

4. PVFS is not an uncommon illness, with at least 1.3 per 1000 of the population being affected. In one study, 71% of general practitioners accepted the existence of PVFS.

5. Patients need to understand their illness and change their lifestyle to increase their chances of recovery.

Important facts

Since 1985 (first edition of this book), management of patients has greatly improved. The illness is common, and becoming more recognised. However, patients still need to take responsibility for their behaviour. A change of lifestyle is usually accompanied by recovery.

CHAPTER FOUR
SYMPTOMS

What a patient complains of (his/her symptoms) is a personal, subjective opinion. It is difficult for other people to fully appreciate the severity of the symptoms. A description of "a tickling sensation" was so severe for one patient that it was "torture", whereas, another patient described the same sensation as "a relaxing feeling".

VIRAL INFECTIONS

Viruses are very much smaller than bacteria, and cannot be seen through a normal microscope. There are thousands of viruses and each year many more are discovered. Some infect animals and plants and others infect human beings. In different countries of the world (especially the tropics), different viruses are found. Viruses can only replicate (or multiply) within living cells. They hijack a living cell's machinery and utilise it to produce viral offspring. **The statement: "just a viral infection" is a gross underestimation of the sophistication of viral infections.**

VIRAL-LIKE INFECTIONS

PVFS can be produced by many infections, but the majority are probably caused by viruses. As stated before, the **"viral" in PVFS refers to the fact that the vast majority of patients remember a "viral-like" illness** at the onset with fever, muscle pain and malaise. Causes of viral-like infections are shown in Figure 4.

Bacteria are common causes of infection. Lyme borreliosis is considered in chapter 15. **Brucellosis is an important infection which causes PVFS.** (*Brucella abortus* from cattle, *B.melitensis* from goats and sheep and *B.suis* from pigs). Diagnosis of chronic brucellosis can be difficult and antibiotic treatment is less effective. **Protozoal infections especially toxoplasma may also cause PVFS.** It is estimated that 5% of PVFS is caused by toxoplasma. Infection is acquired directly or indirectly from cat's faeces. Thus, cat litter trays and unwashed vegetables from contaminated soil or sand pits are major sources of infection. Indirect infection may be acquired by consumption of undercooked meat or by not washing hands after handling contaminated meat. Antibiotic therapy is only indicated in a small number of patients with chronic toxoplasmosis.

Fungal infections may produce a viral-like illness, and some fungal infections may produce PVFS. **Fungal infections probably play a more common role as a secondary complication of PVFS.** Thus, individuals who are ill with PVFS may be more susceptible to fungal infections such as *Candida albicans.* Treatment of such a secondary infection may improve the PVFS but would not cure it.

VIRAL-LIKE INFECTIONS

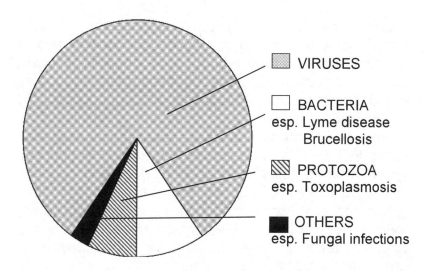

Figure 4 Viral-like infections
These are produced mainly by viruses, but also by bacteria and protozoa. Unless detailed laboratory investigations are undertaken, it can be difficult to find specific causes of such illnesses. PVFS does not mean that viruses are the only cause of the disease.

PVFS

PVFS is particularly common after certain viral infections. Thus, **Epstein-Barr virus** which causes infectious mononucleosis (commonly called glandular fever) is characterised by a sore throat, enlargement of the lymph nodes in the neck, a prolonged fever and malaise with fatigue. A popular description of **infectious mononucleosis** is "the kissing disease", as infection often occurs from transfer of the virus in saliva during a kiss. Hepatitis A is a common infection of tropical countries and visitors can easily become infected; PVFS is a common complication. Hepatitis C is a recently recognised illness which can be particularly debilitating but is an uncommon cause of PVFS.

Coxsackie infections do not usually produce any symptoms, but sometimes a variety of syndromes may develop. Acute infection may affect the brain (with headache, vomiting, pain in the eyes when looking at lights, and stiffness of the neck and spine), heart (with severe pains in the left chest) and chest muscles **(Bornholm's disease).** Bornholm is a Danish island where the disease was first described in 1872. Nearly a quarter of the island's inhabitants developed the illness after attending a wedding feast. One 10 year old boy "suddenly threw himself down on the lawn, screaming" because of the pain in his side. Similar outbreaks **(epidemic myalgia)** have been described all over the world, and in America the disease was called **"devil's grip"** because of the severity of the pain. Coxsackie infection is spread from the faeces of infected persons. **The outlook is good and patients do not die from the disease,** although during the illness they may feel that they are about to die. The acute disease often only lasts a few days, but occasionally persists for a few weeks. In only a **very small minority** is there persistence of symptoms and development of PVFS.

From the above, it is apparent that many infections are not new diseases. **What is new is the recognition that in a minority of patients, PVFS develops.** This concept that many infections may rarely produce PVFS was stated in the first edition of this book. However, it has only recently been observed by others[5]. The symptoms of PVFS are many and varied. **The most common complaint is fatigue, from which the syndrome derives its name.** Other symptoms are best divided into: general, muscular, vascular, neurological, gastrointestinal, cardiac and respiratory. This division is artificial and many symptoms overlap the divisions, for example tiredness is a general symptom but may be related to muscular weakness or neurological anxiety about being tired.

Another common complaint is the feeling of ill-health (malaise) which may accompany excessive tiredness and exhaustion. **In some patients their inactivity is accompanied by increased sweating, and worse, well-wishers saying that they should rest more as they were sweating.** Explanations by the patient are regarded with disbelief. After all, to the average citizen, one sweats when one is active. **Muscular problems are present in the majority of patients.** There can be muscle pain, weakness, tremors, twitches, heaviness, cramp, burning and easy fatigue or a persistent feeling of unsteadiness. **It is likely that there is both muscle and brain dysfunction.**

Abnormal vascular function is quite common. **Cold or very warm hands and feet can be confusing, paradoxical complaints.** An explanation may be related to sex as women often complain of the cold, whereas men more commonly have warm extremities. Patients may also change their complaints. Thus patients may complain of great heat and ask for all the windows to be left open and the heating turned off in the middle of winter. A few months later these same patients may require four blankets in the middle of summer because of the cold. In both sexes, friends may comment that there is loss of colour in the face. **This could be described as "pallor" or even a "grey, mask-like appearance".**

Neurological symptoms are probably the most diverse, and perhaps the most worrying. Headaches may last several weeks and cause the patient much anxiety. Light-headedness, dizziness, sensitivity to temperature, ringing in the ears, blurred vision and sore eyes are common complaints. Difficulty in speaking or finding the right words, poor memory, tingling in the limbs or loss of sensation in different parts of the body are less common.

Gastrointestinal symptoms are very common and in many cases may be related to the development of food intolerance or allergy. A feeling of not being hungry (anorexia) can occur on its own or is sometimes related to patients' frustration with their illness. Diarrhoea can vary between a few extra stools each day to "streaming, almost like water with a horrible smell". **Many complain of alternating diarrhoea and constipation.** Abdominal pain and distension are common and may be a result of gastrointestinal muscle dysfunction.

Cardiac and respiratory complaints can be a part of the acute illness, and persist as part of PVFS. Pains in the chest, awareness of the heart beating **(palpitations)** and difficulty in breathing **(dyspnoea)** are the usual symptoms. Attacks may not be predictable, but in some patients, particular events or times of the day (especially late at night) are associated with most attacks.

SUMMARY

1. There are thousands of viruses and each year more are discovered.

2. PVFS is usually caused by viruses, but also by bacteria, protozoa and fungi.

3. Symptoms of PVFS are many and varied. Any system of the body may be involved. Fatigue is the most common complaint, but fatigue on its own is insufficient to make the diagnosis.

Important facts

Many infections may cause PVFS. Any part of the body may be involved and symptoms may change. Patients should not be worried about the wide range of complaints in this illness.

CHAPTER FIVE
MANAGEMENT

The first objective in management is to obtain a diagnosis. Many people make the mistake of thinking PVFS patients have only fatigue. Fatigue is a common complaint of patients with psychiatric disorders, and this is why some think PVFS is a psychiatric illness. Before a diagnosis of PVFS can be made, **all of the other causes of fatigue (Figure 5) have to be excluded.**

DIAGNOSTIC CRITERIA

In the past, there have been attempts at establishing diagnostic criteria for the disease (Oxford, London, Australian criteria). These were mainly criteria for research so that the same group of patients was being studied. **These criteria did not help the prompt diagnosis of patients** as, for example, they required the patient to be ill for 6 months. My criteria require illness for only 3 months, by which time infections require the approach as stated in this book. More recently, the Canadian guidelines are an excellent example of the problem: they are 150 pages long; require 6 months of

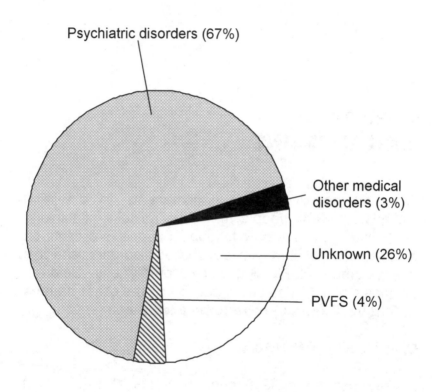

Psychiatric disorders (67%)

Other medical disorders (3%)

Unknown (26%)

PVFS (4%)

Figure 5 Causes of fatigue
If only the complaint of fatigue is considered, the majority of patients (67%) will have a psychiatric disorder. However, if a strict definition of PVFS is used only 4% of patients with fatigue will have PVFS. A small number (3%) will have another medical disorder, but for many, no cause is found (25%)[6].

illness; require the presence of pain; and omit important investigations. I believe that my diagnostic criteria are still valuable and useful.

Diagnosis of PVFS
Patients must fulfil the definition and have supporting evidence of PVFS[7]:

Definition
The patient with Post Viral Fatigue Syndrome:
- has had generalised, relapsing fatigue exacerbated by minor exercise causing disruption of usual daily activities (at least 50%) for three months.
- complains of prominent disturbance of concentration and/or short term memory impairment.
- has no other *obvious*, organic causes for a similar syndrome.

Supporting evidence
(at least four items from sections A, B and C):
A. History
Patient well before illness; an initiating viral illness (clinical description/viral serology); myalgia; gastrointestinal disturbance; headaches; depression; tinnitus; paraesthesiae; sleep disturbance; cardiovascular complaints; adverse effect of alcohol; adverse effect of heat.
B. Clinical
Lymphadenopathy; localised muscle tenderness; pharyngitis.

C. Laboratory
Evidence of viral infection; abnormalities in immune function.

It is important that the doctor takes a detailed history and makes a full clinical examination. **Several hundred conditions may produce a similar illness** and it is the doctor's responsibility to exclude any other cause of the patient's complaints.

INVESTIGATIONS

Several initial investigations apply to most patients. **There are non-specific changes** which show that the patient has an infection, but there is no indication of the cause of the infection. Secondly, **there are specific changes** indicative of a particular infection. These are usually antibodies which are produced by the body's lymphocytes to kill the infecting organism. **Unfortunately, there can be great difficulty in diagnosing viral infections.** Problems often occur in patients who are ill for months or years. Attempts to grow the virus are usually futile because in only a few cases are symptoms due to continuing viral infection.

In individual patients, it may be appropriate to attempt to identify specific causes of PVFS. A respiratory infection screen and Coxsackie neutralisation tests should be done. If tick bites are common, Lyme borreliosis should be excluded. In patients with recurrent sore throats, Epstein-Barr virus infection should be considered. Persisting lymphadenopathy is also a feature of Epstein-Barr virus infection or toxoplasmosis. In patients with abnormal liver function tests, Hepatitis C should be excluded. If facilities are available, it can be useful to demonstrate immunological abnormalities. **The diagnosis of chronic bacterial, protozoal and fungal infections may be equally difficult.** Again, investigations may have to be done in specialised laboratories. Thus, PVFS is diagnosed by the characteristic history, excluding other causes of the patient's symptoms, and finding viral or immunological evidence of a past infection.

TIME TO RECOVERY

The length of time that symptoms persist is a constant source of anxiety for patients, their relatives and their friends. Most people's experience of a viral disease is of an acute illness, lasting a few weeks. **Whereas this is absolutely true, equally true is that most people's experiences are very limited.** The medical literature has numerous descriptions of individual cases and of outbreaks of illness where viral illnesses can persist for years. It is reasonable to expect to win the lottery. **It is unreasonable to plan your life in the expectation of rapid recovery, or winning a fortune.** Such expectations put a strain on a patient's recovery, and worse when they do not materialise, depression can follow. **A superior approach to the problem is to plan a change of lifestyle and a gradual recovery over months or years.** Support from relatives and friends on this basis is much more constructive, and better still, such help reinforces any progress that is made.

I find that when patients follow the plan in this book, they recover on average 10% (1/10) every two months. The **very best patients can recover 20% (2/10) in two**

months. Most patients take 10-12 months to recover. Often there is good progress until 5/10 and then the patient gets stuck. The patient is feeling so much better than 1/10 that there is an acceptance of this level of recovery. Next, some patients get stuck at 7/10. If patients can pass 7/10, there is usually complete recovery.

Therefore, **the vast majority of patients recover within the first year.** Of the remainder, most recover within two years. If a patient is ill for a longer time, the chances of full recovery progressively decreases. **This is largely because the length of illness is a reflection of a patient's ability to change his/her lifestyle.** The longer a person has been trying to pass the test, the chances of success becomes less. Nevertheless, **it is possible for patients to recover even after many decades of illness.**

Why do people find it so difficult to accept that recovery may take years, and that some people may never totally recover? Everyone would understand gradual improvement after a serious car accident. If there is a diagnosis of advanced cancer, any improvement would be looked upon as a miracle. **Attitudes to viral infections are different because there is nothing to see (unlike the car accident), and people's experiences are limited.**

THE SOLUTION

The solution to patients' problems is first to recognise their situation. All patients with PVFS are in vicious circles (Figure 6). A few patients do not recognise that

44

VICIOUS CIRCLES

Figure 6 Vicious circles
Patients' under-performance in many areas can produce
tremendous stress.   This stress produces further, reduced
performance. Patients have to get out of these vicious circles.

they are in such circles, and many would refuse to consider the possibility that such situations may exist. **The recognition of the existence of these vicious circles is often the key to developing a plan for recovery from PVFS.** A major objective of the plan is to remove patients from these vicious circles.

Many patients with PVFS were high achievers before their illness and **one great problem is the lack of achievement that comes with the illness.** The isolation of minimal activity, little money, and no social life is difficult to cope with, especially as many patients were previously "the life and soul" of parties. Close relationships, especially sexual ones, undergo tremendous strain. Fortunately, most patients eventually recognise that their current position is one of vicious circles. However, another difficulty is that **they see no way of getting out of these circles.** The solutions in this book will get patients out of their vicious circles.

Better recovery does not mean immediate recovery. There is **only** slow, gradual recovery from PVFS. What can be learnt is that if life is lived in the same way as before the viral illness, recovery will be even slower. **Instead, a change of lifestyle will allow a better and faster recovery,** especially if the change takes into account the different needs of the body after a viral infection. It is hoped that sufficient information will be provided in this book to enable patients to adopt a positive approach to their illness. It is similar but better than having a leg amputated. With one leg, patients have to learn a different approach to life's problems, and eventually hardly notice that they have one leg. **For patients with PVFS, they also have to learn a new**

way of life, but for them eventually things return to normal – their leg regrows!!

SUMMARY

1.   Symptoms of PVFS are many and varied. Any system of the body may be involved. Diagnosis of PVFS should be made by a doctor. A strict definition of PVFS should be used, and routine investigations undertaken.

2.   Patients may take years to recover and should plan for gradual recovery rather than instant cure. This is a firm basis for asking for support from relatives and friends.

3.   The solution to patients' problems is first to recognise their situation. Patients are in many vicious circles. When this is acknowledged, a plan for recovery can be developed.

4.   Better recovery is only slow and gradual. It is not sufficient to read this book; patients must change their behaviour.

Important facts

PVFS complaints can involve any part of the body. The diagnosis must be made by a doctor. Patients should get out of vicious circles, and change their lifestyles.

CHAPTER SIX
FIRST STEP:
REMAIN SANE

In the fourth edition of this book, the title of this chapter was "Mind out". This was chosen as the mind is the part of the person that is responsible for thoughts, feelings and intentions. The mind also plays a major part in determining a patient's recovery from PVFS. "Mind out" was a good choice as it means "to be careful" or "pay attention", and is what is required of PVFS patients. In the third edition of this book, the title of this chapter was "Remain sane". **Some readers have felt that this title "shocked" them into thinking about their sanity** and their illness. They felt that this was better. This is why I have chosen to return to this title. To remain sane, patients have to understand their illness, and the relationship with psychiatric disorders and associated conditions.

THE ILLNESS

The most common complaints of PVFS patients are fatigue (asthenia) or tiredness. Associated complaints are malaise and weakness (lassitude). Malaise is a general feeling of ill-health. Weakness is the patient's perception that the muscles have reduced strength. **Fatigue is a state of tiredness in which the patient lacks energy and is unable to do much.** Obviously, fatigue and weakness blend into each other, and sometimes they cannot be separated. **Of patients' complaints, fatigue and weakness are the most frequent and complex.** For many doctors, these symptoms may also suggest psychiatric illness. **Many PVFS patients are referred to a psychiatrist.**

There is the age old conundrum: what came first, the chicken or the egg? Patients' emotional state can influence the function of their immune system. **Therefore, patients' emotional state may predispose them to a viral infection, and to delayed recovery from that infection.** It may also be argued that patients were previously well and that it is the illness itself which has produced the emotional abnormalities. Further, social and work consequences of the illness can produce such effects, even if the initial illness does not. The PVFS patient has to cope with the aftermath of a viral infection and emotions; **what came first is academic.**

PSYCHIATRIC DISORDERS

Many PVFS patients develop some of the complaints of psychiatric disorders. The nature of PVFS, the loss of good health, the length of the illness and the lack of quick treatments may all combine to adversely effect patients. **Patients should be aware that there are several time bombs: depression, anxiety, paranoia and suicide.** In the studies where 75% of hospital PVFS patients have a psychiatric disorder, the patients have usually been ill for years; in studies of recently-ill PVFS patients, the presence of a psychiatric disorder is considerably less and most are emotionally well[8]. We found that if patients are treated early in their illness, there is a better prognosis.

1. Depression
Depression or unhappiness is a common human emotion. It is a normal, healthy reaction to some of life's problems. It is only a medical problem when it is uncontrollable or if there is no obvious cause for the depression. Thus, for PVFS patients, **it is not abnormal to be occasionally depressed about tiredness and easy fatigue, indeed it is normal and even necessary.** But, if this depression occurs all the time, then, it is abnormal.

2. Anxiety
Anxiety is a feeling of unease, apprehension, uncertainty and fear. With anxiety, unlike ordinary fear, the unease is out of proportion to the reason for the fear. Thus, PVFS patients may be anxious about going shopping or being in large crowds. Indeed, in such situations many have panic attacks. **Panic attacks are sudden, short-lived anxiety attacks.** Although this may be difficult to understand, I believe that they are due to the increased concentration required for such activities, and the patients' realisation that they may not be able to cope. Good examples of such activities are driving, shopping or going to parties. **Such patients only cope with these situations when they start to recover.**

3. Paranoia

Paranoia is the development of feelings of suspicion and wariness of those around. There is a tendency to blame others and gradually delusions develop, with feelings of self-importance and entitlement. PVFS patients find it difficult to understand how those around can have only a very limited interest in their predicament. Patients can have no one that they can talk to about their illness. **Patients then become suspicious of those around, imagining that others are speaking about them.** There is increased wariness in relationships and gradual deterioration of friendships.

4. Suicide

Fortunately for most patients, this is only a fleeting thought. Patients' lives can become so disrupted and disturbed that there may be little attraction in life. Each day, patients get up hoping to be cured. When this does not happen, they can feel abandoned and without hope. Their friends and relatives do not appreciate their frustration. They can become isolated and lonely. **The world has little attraction.** In this situation, **contemplation of suicide is not surprising and can even appear to be a logical solution to many problems.** Fortunately, the vast majority of patients reject suicide. This is probably because PVFS patients usually have a great zest for life, and suicidal feelings can quickly pass.

ASSOCIATED DISORDERS

Patients should be aware that there are several disorders associated with PVFS (Figure 7). Knowledge of these relationships is valuable in reassuring patients that the wrong diagnosis has not been made. For example, patients may feel that all of their complaints are due to irritable bowel syndrome or primary fibromyalgia syndrome. **Whereas PVFS and these conditions may have some common factors, there are different illnesses.** Few patients will have two illnesses. However, some patients may go on to develop another illness after recovering from PVFS. The doctor has the difficult task of making the diagnosis as these conditions are managed differently.

1. Tension Headaches
These are believed to be a result of stress on an individual. In individuals with tension headaches, fatigue is usually a minor complaint, and these patients can be completely well in the absence of stress. PVFS patients may develop such headaches and they may last weeks, and the headaches can be very resistant to treatment. **However, in PVFS the headaches are principally a result of over-activity,** although stress may be a contributing factor. Headaches in PVFS are managed symptomatically and with bed rest.

2. Irritable Bowel Syndrome
The situation here is quite different. **A large number of PVFS patients have abdominal complaints, especially alternating diarrhoea and constipation.** In addition, abdominal pain, "fullness" or "bloating" after a meal are

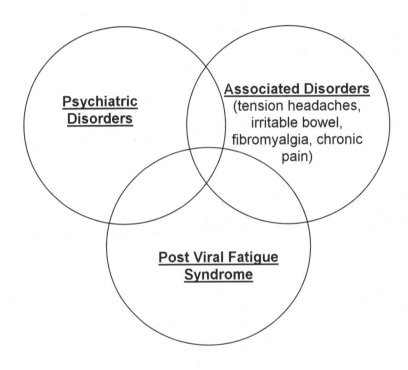

Figure 7   PVFS and other associated conditions
Patients with tension headaches, irritable bowel syndrome, fibromyalgia syndrome or chronic pain syndrome may develop PVFS. This is probably because infections can occur in any group of patients.   Similarly, PVFS patients may go on to develop these other conditions.

common. In many patients the muscles in the gastrointestinal tract are probably affected.

3. Primary Fibromyalgia Syndrome
This is an illness in which there are very tender areas in specific sites in a patient's body. The characteristic pattern of tender points is diagnostic and this condition is easily separated from PVFS. The illness is usually chronic and there is evidence that many patients have an abnormal sleeping pattern[9]. Medical practitioners must differentiate these two illnesses. **It is important to distinguish this condition from PVFS as the management is different.** Whereas in PVFS, patients have to remain within their energy limits. (see later chapters), patients with primary fibromyalgia syndrome should be counselled to live with their pain. **Increasing exercise may be helpful** and more attention must be paid to sleeping patterns.

4. Chronic Pain Syndrome
In this disorder, pain is the major complaint and fatigue is secondary. To make the diagnosis, several criteria have to be met. For the patient, management is different. **The aim is to make the patient become accustomed to the pain,** to recognise that it is not sinister and to learn to work through the pain. This again is a situation where exercise can be encouraged and can be a help.

MANAGEMENT

I believe that all the scientific evidence suggests that psychiatric disorders are not the cause of PVFS. Nevertheless, there is a complex relationship between PVFS, psychiatric disorders and some other associated conditions (Figure 7). **Patients with PVFS may go on to develop these disorders, and patients with these disorders may develop PVFS.** Specific management of the disorders mentioned in this chapter is different from PVFS. Obviously, patients with PVFS and another disorder, have to have both conditions managed. This is not an uncommon finding in medicine, especially in older patients. In cases where the diagnosis is in doubt, **there can be a trial of treatment.** The patient is managed as in this book and the results examined. If there is no improvement in 2-3 months, then PVFS is not the diagnosis. However, if there is significant improvement, PVFS is the diagnosis.

DISHEARTENED

A major factor in patients is that they become disheartened with their disease. Fears that their diagnosis is not right can make matters worse. And if they develop another illness, there can be total disillusionment. **To remain sane, patients have to have a good understanding of their illness, and that they may develop other disorders.** Good days and bad days are a part of the illness. On good days, patients can be high on top of a mountain. On bad days, descent into the sea of disheartened can take hours (Figure 8). Therefore, patients should plan for bad days. **We all have things that cheer us up and patients can take early action** to prevent themselves falling into the sea of disheartened. These actions seem so trivial that they are often not even considered. **Yet, this approach works. The essence is to recognise that _early_ action is required.** Patients should put aside a variety of obstacles to being disheartened (Figure 8). These may

HIGH

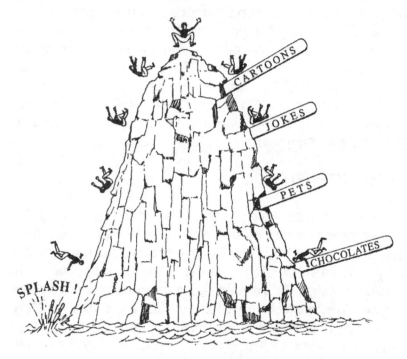

SEA OF DISHEARTENED

Figure 8 Sea of disheartened
Many patients tumble down from a high at the top of a mountain into the sea of disheartened. This need not happen. Instead, a choice of cartoons, jokes, pets and even food (such as chocolate) can be effective obstacles to feeling disheartened.

56

be: favourite videos (especially cartoons); jokes that have been particularly funny; pets whose antics make you laugh; or, food that makes you happy, even if it is a special chocolate. Remember that prevention is better than a cure.

Recordings on a tape recorder or video of favourite programmes on radio or television are particularly useful. However, similar enjoyment may be obtained from looking at travel brochures, or reading a passage in a book about an odd place or situation. **Patients who are prone to becoming disheartened should collect things that make them laugh.** The importance of laughter must not be underestimated. **When people laugh their bodies function more effectively.** There is evidence that the immune system is more effective, with greater circulation of natural killer cells. These cells are the body's first response to infections. Laughter can stimulate their production. **Some patients should laugh for five minutes, three times a day. It sounds a bit odd, but it works.** It does not matter if laughter is real or simulated.

For most patients prone to be disheartened, these remedies can prevent deep depression. However for some patients, antidepressants are required. Patients sometimes feel that they should not accept such therapy. They may feel that if they take antidepressants, it will prove that their illness is due to depression or that they may become "hooked" on tablets. This is unlikely. **Antidepressants are a valuable support for patients and they should be used.**

SUMMARY

1. PVFS patients have to believe in themselves. They must care for themselves to remain sane.

2. Fatigue (asthenia) or tiredness are common complaints of patients with psychiatric disorders. PVFS patients are easily distinguished from psychiatric patients by the case definition of PVFS.

3. Psychiatric disorders (depression, anxiety, paranoia, suicide) are often a result of the illness. PVFS is not caused by psychiatric disorders.

4. Tension headaches, irritable bowel syndrome, primary fibromyalgia syndrome and chronic pain syndrome are associated with PVFS.

5. Patients should adopt strategies to prevent being disheartened. Antidepressants can be of great value to some patients.

```
┌─────────────────────────────────────┐
│                                     │
│           Important facts           │
│                                     │
│  To remain sane, the patient needs to │
│  have knowledge of the illness, its │
│  effects and associated conditions. It is │
│  possible to avoid being disheartened │
│  by being prepared.                 │
│                                     │
└─────────────────────────────────────┘
```

Important facts

To remain sane, the patient needs to have knowledge of the illness, its effects and associated conditions. It is possible to avoid being disheartened by being prepared.

CHAPTER SEVEN

SECOND STEP:
ACQUIRE KNOWLEDGE

Brian was a man who did not like to spend money. One day, before taking the bus, he asked the conductor how much it was to the bus terminal.

"Fifty pence" said the conductor.

This was too much for Brian, so he decided to run behind the bus for the next two stops, and then asked:

"How much is it to the bus terminal now?"

"Eighty pence" said the conductor, "You're running in the wrong direction."

Many patients, even with the very best intentions, are running in the wrong direction. Most PVFS patients have not had a simple explanation of what they have to do. Many are faced with too complicated advice. Alternatively, it is: "there is nothing to be done" or "the disease will burn itself out". **These are all wrong.** PVFS patients need to acquire knowledge of their illness to recover. This is because their illness is individual and only the patient can truly understand the disabling effects of the illness.

GENERAL AND SELF KNOWLEDGE

From newspapers or magazines, general knowledge of the illness is relatively easy to acquire. At this stage, **patients feel that if they become more knowledgeable, they may be accused of wanting to be ill.** Sadly, the effects of the illness make people defensive. **Patients' perceptions of the illness can be illogical.** Many times patients have admitted to me that they did not like the diagnosis of PVFS and would rather if I said that they had cancer. **This attitude is totally different to the general public's belief that PVFS patients would choose the diagnosis of PVFS rather than be well.** This is yet another example of the divide between reality and its perception. Patients need to become serious. They need to have more detailed knowledge.

Self knowledge of the illness is not easily acquired and involves a medium degree of difficulty. Patients will have to try and understand all of their symptoms. They will need to read a book about their illness. With this greater knowledge, patients will be able to see their illness as a whole. **Sadly many patients see their illness as only bad news** (Figure 9). It requires a great effort to even start to look for information with this attitude . in mind. **Other patients are happy to learn about their illness, but refuse to learn about themselves.** Often, patients hate what they have become. They feel that if they acquire more knowledge of themselves, their worse

PATIENT'S LIFE

Figure 9   Patient's life
Many patients can see only the bad news in their life. Illness
has created limited vision. Recovery depends on patients
being able to see their whole life. Many will then recognise
that there is more good news than bad news.

fears will be confirmed. **Their worse fears are usually that they would not be able to be active again.**

Patients remember their past life and cannot bear to look at their present position. **They are essentially mourning the death of their past existence.** As with all mourning, their ability to face the facts is limited. They refuse to accept that their past existence is over. Yet, for recovery, **patients need to understand what is happening and recognise their mourning.** My book, "Climbing Out of the Pit of Life" (Dodona Books), was written to help patients come to terms with great loss.

Fortunately, for many patients **it will be recognised that they often lived on adrenaline**. As with all drugs, it can be addictive. Yet, it is possible to be happy and content without adrenaline. One patient said that he was happy only when car racing. Then, he felt no pain, nor tiredness. Usually this was followed by two weeks in bed – the after effects of the adrenaline. Equally important are the symptoms. Although patients realise that they have similarities in their symptoms, there are also differences. **It is very unusual to find two patients with exactly the same complaints.** This does not mean that different patients have different illnesses. Instead, it is that a patient's complaints are individual. It is important to identify these individual complaints so that solutions can be found. Even when patients have the same complaints, the solution may not be the same.

DAILY DIARY

Most patients were previously well-organised individuals who prided themselves on their abilities to solve problems. Sadly, when memory and/or concentration are affected, a once efficient individual may behave like a headless chicken. When people succeed in life, they often have an edge. It may be in ability, organisation or luck. Usually success is a reflection of accentuating one's strengths and minimising the effects of one's weaknesses. **It therefore makes sense to compensate for poor memory by keeping a daily diary.**

A daily diary is very hard to keep. Many patients and their relatives regard a daily diary as "patients wallowing in their illness." I cannot accept this argument. Recovery depends on knowledge; and without a diary, how do you know if you are going in the right direction? Patients often reply that they know that they are getting worse. **If patients are getting worse, they are obviously going in the wrong direction.** The daily diary has several problems:

	Problem	Degree of Difficulty
1.	Desire	High
2.	Format	Low
3.	Regularity	Medium
4.	Content	Low
5.	Precision	Medium
6.	Scoring system	High

For an ill individual, the above may appear formidable. Yet, overall it is not a difficult task. **I have not found a patient who cannot keep a good diary.** Indeed, many children can be taught to produce excellent diaries. However, patients must first want to help themselves.

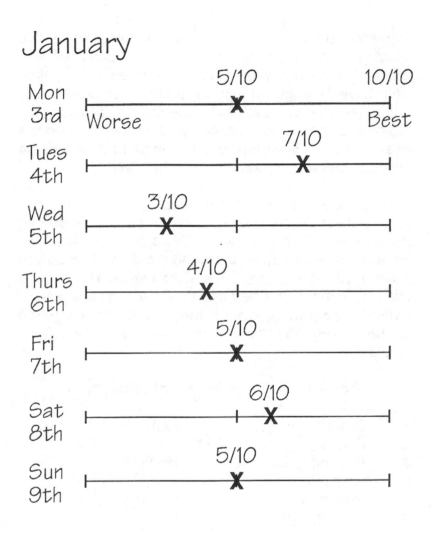

January

Mon 3rd — 5/10 — 10/10 — Worse / Best

Tues 4th — 7/10

Wed 5th — 3/10

Thurs 6th — 4/10

Fri 7th — 5/10

Sat 8th — 6/10

Sun 9th — 5/10

Figure 10 Left-hand page of the diary
One page is used for each week. On the left-hand page of the
exercise book, daily scores are kept of how the patient feels
on a scale of 1-10.

Mon   Sleep 12hr. Hospital. Travel (2hrs)
       Sleep afternoon (3hrs) TV (1hr) Bad day.

Tues   Sleep 14hrs. Short walk (1/2hr) Visitors x2
       Telephone x3. TV (3hrs) Good day.

Wed   Sleep 8hrs Bad night. Very tired
       Back to bed (6hrs) TV (2hrs) Terrible.

Thurs Sleep 8hrs. Disturbed night. Read (1hr)
       Unwind (x2) TV (2hrs) Boredom (X2) Better.

Fri   Sleep 12hrs. Read (2hrs) Unwind (x2)
       Telephone (x2) Boredom (x3) Boring day.

Sat   Sleep 14hrs. Argument with mother (11/2hrs)
       Shopping (2hrs) Telephone (x2) Fair day.

Sun   Sleep 10hrs. Church (2hrs) Visitors x2
       Unwind (x1) TV (3hrs) Average day.

Figure 11 Right-hand page of the diary
One page is used for each week. On the right-hand page, two lines describe the patient's day. Do not write in sentences. Record hours of sleep and relaxation, activities, visitors, telephone calls, problems and how you feel.

1. Desire

Many patients initially accept the need for a diary, but after a week they cannot be bothered. **I feel that the diary is so important that I would refuse to see a patient who did not keep a diary.** Apart from the reasons given above, I can tell how a patient has been over six weeks in 5 minutes if the patient has a diary. If there is no diary, the same information takes 45-60 minutes to acquire. The desire to keep a diary has a high degree of difficulty because patients have no energy to keep a diary, and they feel that their lives are so boring that there is no help in a diary. Patients often say "every day is exactly the same," "all I do is rest" or "I have no energy to do anything." Yet, some patients get better and others do not. **In patients who are getting worse, there are usually several things that they are doing wrong.** The fastest way for me to find out what they are doing wrong is to examine a daily diary.

The daily diary that I like takes 3 minutes per day to keep. This is not a large amount of time. I believe that if patients cannot give 3 minutes per day for their diary, it is not surprising that they are not getting better. **The diary must also be written by the patient.** I am often told "my wife/husband will do the diary" or "my mother/father is good at writing." **However, I always insist on the patient doing the diary.** Even young children can be taught to keep a useful diary. It is also a measure of the patient's commitment to getting better.

2. Format

The format of the diary is depicted in Figures 10 and 11. **A school exercise book is best as you can write on both sides of the paper.** I do not like photocopying the format. Although photocopying reduces some work, it is not as easy to refer to or use. **Two pages should be used for each week: one page for scores (Figure 10) and the next page for the patient's activities (Figure 11).** Sometimes patients feel that they want to write more. This is good but it is important that this diary be on one page, and often patients who like to write more will keep two diaries.

3. Regularity
The format of my diary is designed to be simple. It can be done even though patients are very ill. Many patients remark at how simple the diary appears. The diary can be very difficult for an individual who is in relapse. **A daily diary is the cornerstone for better recovery.** Yet, with a relapse, there can be blank pages, patients will reply with indignation: "I did nothing, so I wrote nothing!" This is not good enough. **I only require two lines each day, but I need these two lines every day of the year.** To be of benefit, the diary **must** be done every day.

4. Content
Although of low difficulty, many patients find this is a problem. Many patients remember how active they were, and feel that in comparison there is nothing to write. This does not deal with the problem. **The problem is simply that without detailed daily information, a patient's chance of recovery is greatly diminished.** Patients should have a systematic approach to the content of a diary. Firstly, there is no need to write in sentences. It is only 2-3 lines and therefore it needs to contain as much information as possible. State the important facts first: hours of sleep, hours of relaxation and if you are having a

period (menstruation). Next, record how you have spent your time in hours of television, radio, reading newspapers or books; and record your number of visitors and telephone calls. You can use abbreviations, e.g. TV for television, or your own system. Lastly, say how you feel (happy, unhappy, good, bad, etc). **Do not become discouraged with your diary.** With time, you will develop an understanding of what should be in the diary. Like many skills in life, a diary takes time and effort.

5. Precision
Many diaries start off being emotional rather than precise. Frequent comments are: "This is hell on earth," "I am about to die," and "When will I find peace?" However, to be of value, a diary needs to be precise. So, more useful comments would be: "I can't get out of bed," "I can only walk 100 yards," "I had diarrhoea ten times today," or "My headache lasted 12 hours." **A precise diary allows comparison over time.** One or two years later, patients may be able to go back and see how they were. I am always surprised that patients are quite happy to say to me: "I have not been well for years and it is getting worse each year." Yet, when I asked them when it started, there is usually a blank stare. When I ask how it has got worse over each six-month period, there is a look of astonishment that I might require such information. **Without such information it is impossible to predict the future progress of the illness.**

6. Scoring system
This is the most difficult part of the diary. Patients have so many difficulties with this aspect of the diary that it deserves a special section with greater detail.

SCORING SYSTEM

It takes time for patients to have an overall impression of how they are. First, patients feel differently at different times of the day. Some are worse in the morning; others are worse at night. Some patients often feel that they should score themselves in the morning, afternoon, evening and at night. This is too complicated. **Patients should learn to develop an overall average score for the day.**

The scoring system is:

Score   **Effects**
1.   Severe symptoms at rest. In bed all day.
2.   Moderate to severe symptoms at rest. Feels unable to work. Concentration and activity severely affected.
3.   Moderate symptoms at rest. Feels unable to work full-time. Activities severely affected.
4.   Mild symptoms at rest. Feels just able to work full-time but not in a physical or stressful job. Frequent rest/relaxation needed.
5.   Very mild symptoms at rest. Moderate to severe symptoms with exercise or activity. Feels able to work full-time, but not in a physical or stressful job. Social life restricted.
6.   Very mild or no symptoms at rest. Moderate symptoms with exercise. Feels able to work full-time, but not in a physical job. Social life affected.
7.   Very mild or no symptoms at rest. Mild symptoms, with exercise. Feels able to work full-time but not in a physical job. Some social life.

8. No symptoms at rest. Very mild or no symptoms with some exercise. Feels able to work full-time in a reasonably active job. Some social life.
9. No symptoms at rest. Few symptoms with exercise. Feels able to work full-time in a reasonably active job. More social life.
10. Patient well.

The scoring system is rated as being of high degree of difficulty. This is because there are several problems which patients have:

a) Feel before you do: Scores are what you feel or think that you can do. It is not about what you can do. Many patients do not want to score a number until they can do it; **this is wrong.** You must feel that you might be able to do something for several weeks before you try it.

b) Have before you spend: The left-hand side of the diary is your income and the right-hand side is how you spend it. You must have high scores before you do more. Most patients want to spend it first (on credit) and promise themselves that they will pay it back after the event. **This is wrong.** There is no spending on credit as you are already bankrupt. This strict discipline is critical for recovery.

c) Too much precision: using decimal places (5.1 or 4.35). Patients should stick to whole numbers, occasionally halves or quarters are acceptable.

d) Changes in a week: it is useful to look at a week and see one day that was better or worse than the rest. Thus, to see seven 5's is not as useful as five 5's, one 4

70

and one 6. Overall for the week the score is the same. Do not be afraid of using a range of numbers.

e) Wanting to change past scores: patients often say "last year this time I scored 5, but it was not really a 5, it was a 3; I am now a 5." The score that is correct is the score that you **feel now.** A year from now, if you feel better you should score yourself higher, rather than go back to the diary and change the previous year's scores.

f) Fear of being too optimistic: there is an irrational fear of scoring higher scores. It is not unlike the teacher who cannot give students full marks. The scoring system has guidelines but patients should score themselves relative to the previous days/weeks.

ANSWER QUESTIONS

Patients sometimes feel that they do the diary for my benefit. **It is useful to me, but it should be more useful to the patient.** When the diary scores are bad, patients should do less. Thus the diary scores influence their behaviour in subsequent days. **The diary is a key to answering many questions about a patient's illness.** Not all female patients feel worse during menstruation, but some do and the diary can provide the answer. One patient used the diary to realise that visiting her father made her worse. Another, detected a food allergy. **Patients need to use the diary to learn.**

Keeping such records can be demanding but they are necessary. A detailed diary shows an outsider that you are concerned about your illness and you are trying to be objective. But more important, a diary can be a tremendous boost when you are going through a difficult time. It is reassuring to be able to know how you compare to 1, 3 or 5 years ago. **Most patients over this period will have improved,** although comparisons over shorter periods (weeks or months) may show deterioration. Being objective about one's illness is difficult. It takes time, and one does not know if it is worth it. **But what is the alternative?** To sit around waiting for a miracle? Detailed recording of symptoms is the second step to better recovery from viral infections. Specific knowledge about oneself will allow a change of attitude and lifestyle. **Great strength can come from the realisation that self-help is possible and that many solutions to problems are within one's capabilities.** Whereas recovery may take years, life can be better now.

GET HIGHER SCORES

Many patients feel that they have no control of scores. It is as though they were counting cars passing along a street and had no control of the cars. My approach is to let them feel that they control the traffic lights for the street. They can let no cars pass or choose the rate at which cars pass. **It is a big step when the diary is not just a record but a result of a patient's ability to control his/her behaviour during the day.** Patients have got higher scores from:

a) The future. The discipline of remaining within your energy levels is not easy. But, what is the reason for such discipline? The reason is so that you get better faster. Thus it is important to remind yourself: "I must be disciplined. My future depends on it. **What I do today**

affects what I will be two months from now". The philosophy must be to sacrifice today for tomorrow.

b) Contracts. Making a contract with yourself can be a tremendous boost in controlling diary scores. Say, for example, that you would not go on the computer (or visit your mother) unless you score half a point above your average of the previous month. Do not set too difficult conditions, but they must not be too easy either! If you can **start to enjoy these contracts,** life can become easier. It is not more restrictive than saying you will only have a barbecue on a sunny day.

c) Early stops. The ability to stop before you run out of energy is very hard for most patients. They stay at the party too long or must watch the last half hour of the video. The fact that their minds are totally out of it, unable to concentrate or take part is not considered. Worse, the **after-effects may influence scores for the next week.** It is madness. It is better to adopt an "early stop" approach. As soon as the battery dims, turn the torch off. As soon as you become tired, go to bed.

d) Crisis management. Managing a bad day is crisis management. On bad days, it is important to make yourself laugh several times. Also you must not make bad days worse: it is not worth attempting a trip, difficult meeting or visit on a bad day. Getting better depends on controlling bad days.

e) "Blow outs". In any system, there must be some time for a "blow out". Obviously it is best that these are planned. It is not bad to have a small blow out once a week, and perhaps a bigger indulgence once a month. It is also a nice feeling to plan a small blow out, but not do it. Instead, save it for another time when you might need it more.

SUMMARY

1. Patients often feel that if they acquire too much information about their illness, they may be accused of wanting to be ill.

2. Patients will have to develop general and self-knowledge of their illness. Many mourn their past existence and do not realise that they are mourning.

3. A daily diary allows patients to know if they are making progress. The diary takes 3 minutes per day, and is not a long time for patients to devote to getting better.

4. Ideally, an exercise book should be used with two pages for each week. The daily diary should record the activities in the day, and a scoring system should be used. Scores reflect what you feel and not what you can do. Also, you must have high scores before you do more.

5. A patient can learn from the daily diary. The diary can provide answers to a patient's questions.

6. There are several ways of getting higher scores, and patients must put these into practice.

Important facts

If you are not getting better, you are doing things wrong. The daily diary can tell you what are your mistakes. The time and effort required can answer many of the questions you have on your illness. The scoring system is essential for faster and better recovery.

CHAPTER EIGHT

THIRD STEP: LOSING ENERGY: EXERCISE, STRESS AND RELATIONSHIPS

The key to better recovery is to understand energy. However, **this is the most difficult concept to communicate to patients.** It is like the wind, you can feel it but it is difficult to understand if you want to see it. It was not until the third edition of this book that I found the solution to explaining energy. Now, **I have a four-part strategy for teaching patients:**

1.   Think of energy as money
2.   Stop losing energy
3.   Start gaining energy
4.   Try making energy last

The first two parts will be dealt with in this chapter, but separate chapters will be devoted to gaining energy (Chapter 9) and making energy last (Chapter 10).

ENERGY AS MONEY

The first part of the strategy is to think of energy as money. To get better, patients need to recognise that they cannot use more energy (or money) than they have. If they do, as with money, they will get worse (or go further into debt). Indeed, as patients are ill, they have a massive overdraft at the bank, so they need to save some money (or energy) each day. The first part of the strategy is explained in Figures 12 to 15. **This approach has worked with many patients over decades.**

In time, patients have to develop the ability of looking at all their activities in terms of money. It is not just physical activities, but also mental activities which use up energy. There is only £100 to spend in the day. **I do not care how you spend this money, but I care if you spend more than your £100.** If you want to go for an early morning walk and spend £50, that is fine. But you must remember that you do not have that money (energy) to use later in the day. Thus, it is more sensible to wait until the evening to see how much money you have left over for the walk. **Like money, if you make a note of all you spend, you will be aware of how easy it is to lose money (energy).**

EXERCISE

Exercise itself is a complex subject, and as with religion, it means different things to different people. Many look upon exercise as extreme physical activity, and involves "going for the burn" or passing through a "pain barrier". I prefer the definition of exercise as "exertion of the body". It can be difficult for patients to

Figure 12 Energy as money
Patients should think that before the illness they had £1000 worth of energy for each day. With PVFS, they have £100 of energy for each day. Like people losing their income, there has to be a severe cutback on spending (activities).

Figure 13 Progress on bad days
To make progress, patients have to go to bed with £10
unspent even on bad days. Usually, patients use more money
(or energy) than they have and end up borrowing money.
Doom and disaster follows.

Figure 14 A good day
A good day is like receiving a £500 prize of energy. It is a great boost but must be used wisely. This great opportunity is often wasted.

Figure 15 Progress on good days
To make progress on good days, patients should spend £300 and say that this amount is three times the bad days, and save £200. This repays the debt quicker and leaves something for tomorrow. Instead, **patients usually try to catch up** with activities, spend all of the £500 and end up borrowing more money. Greater doom and disaster are inevitable.

recognise that they previously regarded only a five mile run as exercise, and I regard a 100 yard walk as exercise. The important factor is not the words used but the cost in energy. Thus, it does not matter if you went "shopping", but how much you spent; and there is a big difference between spending £1000 that you can afford and £10 which you cannot afford. **The important lesson for patients is that all exercise uses energy.**

There is the saying that "there are no free dinners". This means that even if something appears to be free, there is a hidden cost or commitment. It is a universal truth. Thus, for all patients, as with money, one must keep a record of outgoings and record all expenditure. **Then, the true cost of exercise and its value can be considered.** Recently, it has been recognised that many individuals can become addicted to exercise. There is an addiction to the post-exercise high caused by endorphins released into the brain. PVFS patients take longer to recover from their training and their performances begin to suffer, often complicated by frequent infections. These individuals need to remember that **you are healthy only if you can recuperate adequately from training.** Fitness is not about training; **fitness is when you recover from training.** Normally, muscles can take 20 hours to repair themselves. In PVFS patients, this time is greatly increased. **It is not surprising that patients cannot easily recover from training.**

1. Type of exercise

The type of exercise is more important than the quantity and duration. **Some exercise uses more money (energy) than others, so that an hour of squash is more exhausting than an hour of walking the dog.**

Similarly, particular muscle groups can become overworked, so that half an hour chopping down a tree can have a more prolonged effect than the same time floating in the swimming pool. Team games in particular may require bursts of physical activity. **In general, the best type of exercise is one in which the exertion is constant, and capable of being controlled by the patient.** Thus, team games are not advisable, as it is usually not possible to go more slowly or stop. The best activity is one in which the patient controls the pace, however slow it may be.

Certain types of exercise, especially social ones tend to occur at the weekends. This can produce more noticeable effects. A patient with two exercise periods a week complained of excessive tiredness on Monday of each week. On further questioning, all of his activity was on Saturday and Sunday. When he changed his pattern to Saturday and Wednesday, his tiredness was dramatically reduced. Muscle groups that were previously well-developed (e.g. arms or legs; right-handedness or left-handedness) tend to be more severely affected. **Similarly, activities that an individual used to be good at are often more tiring than entirely new activities.** Human behaviour is such that when times are bad, there is a tendency to dig-in or fall-back (i.e. repeat current activity or go back to activities in the past). Both of these natural instincts may result in more tiredness than developing a new interest.

In 1985, I said that it can be helpful to look upon the body as a rechargeable battery. Now, many others have copied this analogy because it works! In the early stages of illness, it is a battery that cannot hold its charge for very long. Thus, exercise quickly results in exhaustion, and is followed by a prolonged period during which the body recharges itself. As the illness progresses, the body gradually improves and becomes a battery capable of holding its charge longer. Now, more exercise can be endured. **Exercise does not result in immediate tiredness, but often several days later, and recovery from tiredness is much faster.** Ideally, patients develop a feel for how much activity and the type of activity that can be tolerated. With the simile of the battery, they know how much charge is going to be used with each activity, and what the effects will be. My usual recommendation is that a patient can start to gradually increase activities when they score 8/10 in their daily diary for 3 weeks. However, there are times when they decide to exhaust themselves in the knowledge that recovery may take weeks. These decisions are no worse than someone deciding to finish the punch at a party, **and knowing that there will be a giant hangover for the next day.**

2. Exercise/Rest debate
From the start, there has been a debate on if exercise or rest produces the best results. Exercise has become refined into a graded exercise programme and some look upon "rest" as being in bed all day. My approach is to **stay within your energy limits** until you reach 80% of normal. I do not believe in patients staying in bed all day. If you are in bed you should sleep. Otherwise it is better to get up even if you are only sitting by the bed.

What is the answer to excessive tiredness in PVFS? Two popular suggestions exist. The first is that the body is weak so it tires easily (because of exhaustion) as the patient is unfit. Not surprisingly, many patients conclude that their tiredness is due to them being unfit; and if they became fit again, their tiredness would go away. In PVFS patients, there is no evidence to support this conclusion. **This reasoning applies to those with normal body function. The evidence in PVFS patients is that their body function is abnormal – they are ill.**

In normal muscles, the pain (or the burn) is due to the build up of lactic acid. Exercise gurus say of this: "There is absolutely nothing harmful or dangerous about it. It just slows you down until the oxygen supply is replenished, which is a matter of seconds." There is evidence that PVFS patients have an abnormal lactate response to exercise[10]. This is probably a result of disordered metabolic regulation in the muscles – a result of the viral infection. **Thus, in PVFS patients, the reason for tiredness is both exhaustion and delayed recovery.** Neither are caused by the patient being unfit, but rather, by the muscles behaving abnormally.

Many PVFS patients have abnormal muscle pathology[10,11]. Unfortunately the pathology is non-specific and variable. The fact that not all patients demonstrate the same abnormalities is to be expected as several mechanisms may result in muscle dysfunction. In addition, patients may be at different stages of the illness. More needs to be learnt before muscle abnormalities can be used in diagnosis. Similarly, cardiovascular and genetic abnormalities require further study[12].

Although patients may know that there are muscle abnormalities, **many cannot believe that exercise is not the answer.** As most individuals who develop PVFS were more athletic than normal, it is not surprising that they should look upon exercise as a solution to their problems. **In the past, they remember being fit – a time when they were able to exercise vigorously, and feel the better for it.** So, how can the question of exercise be answered? This is where the diary is very useful. Attempt to relate tiredness (or other symptoms such as muscle pain) over a two month period to physical exertion. In most patients, it is found that mild exercise, such as a 10 minute walk or a 5 minute swim, does not result in symptoms. Whereas a hill walk for more than an hour produces excessive physical tiredness. **With greater exercise other symptoms can also occur,** especially pain or burning in the muscles, diarrhoea, headaches, difficulty in seeing or hearing, and muscle twitches or tremors.

With the help of the diary, one can establish how much exercise can be tolerated and for how long. **The most important realisation is that there is considerable difference in what patients used to be able to do and what they can do now.** For example, one patient enjoyed running 5 miles to work before his illness, but was only able to walk 10 yards without symptoms after his illness started. Many patients ignore their symptoms, and try to do exactly what they were capable of before their illness. The result is predictable, they feel unwell for the next 7-10 days. **Such forlorn attempts to emulate past achievements always take their toll.** Patients must remember that they are ill. If one's leg was in plaster, no one would contemplate running 5 miles.

However, when someone looks normal, it is easy to assume they are well. **The truth is that health is a reflection of what the body is capable of doing.** Well being is not what the body looks as though it can do, or what someone thinks that it should do.

The diary is particularly useful in showing relationships between symptoms and preceding events. It is best not to think of exercise as producing particular symptoms. **Whatever complaint the patient usually has is made worse by excessive exercise.** Exercise is an additional stress to the body and results in symptoms related to the activity, and worsening of existing complaints. Using the analogy of the battery, if the inside car lights are dim because of a poorly-charged battery, matters are made worse when the headlights are put on full-beam. Generally, patients do not benefit from increasing exercise until they are 80% of normal. It is as though the body needs to recover in other ways before exercise can produce a benefit. **The important lesson is that exercise is a great way of losing energy.**

STRESS

Stress is all around us. For PVFS patients, there must be an awareness and understanding of stress. The definition of stress that I like is: **stress is a process in which the resources of the person are matched against the demands of the environment.** In my book, "Unwind" (Dodona Books, 1991), stress management techniques are carefully considered. Put simply, for chronically ill patients to cope with stress requires either reducing the demands of the environment or increasing their resources. **Resources can be increased by sleep**

and relaxation techniques (Chapter 9). To reduce the demands of the environment is much more difficult. Usually such demands are in three main areas: relationships, job and finances. Employment and finances are considered in Chapter 12.

RELATIONSHIPS

We all need relationships. Among PVFS patients, these relationships can be of great value, but they can also be very expensive in their use of energy:

	Relationship	Stress	Energy loss
1.	Friends	Low/Medium	Low/Medium
2.	Relatives	Medium	Medium
3.	Family	High	High
4.	Partners	Very high	Very high

Obviously, a particularly annoying friend or relative can use more energy than a partner. Thus, the energy losses are approximate and are also a reflection of how I believe you should use your energy. **Thus, your partner should have most of your energy, followed by your family and lastly your friends.** Often, there is not enough energy for all, and patients have to choose their priorities. Many patients forget that there is not enough energy for all of their relationships.

One recent recognition is that energy is lost through mental activity. Although physical activity is the usual way money (energy) is spent, money is also lost through mental activity. **Thus, patients may stay in bed all day, but if they are worrying or anxious, energy is used up as if they were active.** Fortunately, mental activity uses energy more slowly than physical activity. This slowness is deceptive and many patients do not recognise that they are using energy. **Mental activities that use up great energy are: anger, hate, frustration, jealousy, depression and anxiety.** Sadly, these emotions are major factors in relationships.

1. Friends

Friends have problems coping with patients who are changed by the illness. It is not uncommon for a patient to say: **"I only started to get better when I lost all of my friends."** This is because friends remember patients as active, productive individuals. Often, these friends were very dependent on patients. As patients still look the same, their friends still have great expectations of patients. **Patients must be prepared to lose friends who are too demanding.**

Fortunately, there are some friendships in which the contributions of both individuals are equal. These relationships are beneficial to the patients, and are the friendships that should be continued. There is a simple test. **One feels better after sharing some time with a good friend.** If you are angry, annoyed or frustrated after being with someone, you should question the relationship. With illness, patients have limited resources. Therefore, it makes sense to only do what is necessary. **If you can only afford to feed yourself, it is not possible for you to feed your friends.** But, one needs social contact, so it is better to choose friends who are happy to pay for their meal. Facing reality can be very difficult. It means that you may have to decide not to support others. **Patients should concentrate on those relationships that are mutually supportive.**

2. Relatives

Whereas we can choose our friends, we cannot choose our relatives. For most patients, this is good news. **Friends often accept you for what you can do, but relatives accept you because you exist.** The support of relatives for the vast majority of patients is overwhelming. **Help and assistance are usually freely given.** Without this support, many patients would have had great difficulties. Sadly, this is not the whole story. There are many instances, especially with a daughter and an older parent, where the relationship is unhealthy. **Several ill patients feel compelled to support an older parent.** Patients feel guilty and that it is their duty. Often, the parent manipulates the patient and makes many unreasonable demands. The patient dreads visiting the parent and feels terrible after each visit. My advice to these patients is simple: **explain the situation to the parent and reduce the contact; do not feel guilty and do not be manipulated.**

Parents have a responsibility to care for their children; **children do not have a responsibility to care for their parents.** If children care for their parents, they should do so willingly and with love and not because of guilt. Many patients have said to me that they hated their parents; yet, they were prepared to care for the parent, thereby prolonging their illness. I have sadly concluded that if a parent has manipulated offspring for 20-30 years, they cannot stop when the offspring becomes ill. **Worse, when the offspring is ill, he/she is least able to withstand the demands of parents.**

90

3. Family

In this section, I am considering the immediate family. **For patients, the family unit can determine whether they recover or not.** The support of the family is invaluable, as the goodwill in the family is usually high. This goodwill is the key to being able to use the resources of the family. **With illness, the patient's role within the family has to change.** No longer is it possible for the mother to do all of the housework, or the father to do the handyman jobs about the house. The whole family have to be recruited to help. Children, even as young as five years, can be taught to be helpful. **The great obstacle is accepting that the job will not be done properly.** However, it is still better for the patient if children only clean the kitchen 60% as well as the patient. **The patient needs to accept this help, and gently teach the children.** I have felt that with time and good teaching, the job can even be done better by the children. With all good teaching, the pupil should eventually perform better than the teacher.

4. Partners

Partners have a heavy, heavy burden. They see loved ones going through dramatic change: the active become inactive; the confident become afraid; the dependable become erratic; tears, anger and frustration become everyday occurrences. For many it can be too much. **Many PVFS patients end up separated or divorced.** However, I am impressed at how many relationships survive and prosper. The relationships that do well have several common characteristics. These characteristics are probably necessary for all good relationships, however, with illness they can become vitally important:

	Characteristic	Difficulty
1.	Mutual respect	Low
2.	Consideration	Low
3.	Understanding	Medium
4.	Common objectives	Medium
5.	Time together	High
6.	Sexual activity	Very high

I have not used love, possibly because it is so hard to define. **If love is present many of the characteristics are also present, and the relationship will be good.** However, in many relationships in which there is said to be love, one finds one partner doing all the loving and the other consenting to be loved. **A good test of a relationship is sexual activity,** and in PVFS patients this has a very high degree of difficulty. **There are substantial differences between men and women.** With men, sexual activity is generally regarded as the main course of a three course meal; without the main course, there is no sustenance. With women, sexual activity is generally regarded as the dessert of a three course meal; sustenance is obtained with the main course, and the dessert is consumed if there is still hunger, time and inclination. **Couples need to rethink their sexual activity depending on which partner is affected.** This is a matter of great importance and cannot be left until a patient recovers.

A good sexual relationship is an aid to recovery, and a poor one is a large hindrance. Success depends on sexual activity when there is energy and the time is right. This usually means that sex is better in the morning or after lunch rather than at night. It should not be rushed, patients need time for arousal. **It is a**

mistake to think of only touching each other during sexual activity. Often, there are good reasons for this, such as a patient being in a lot of pain. However, if there is love, a gentle touch can be a powerful analgesic; cuddles should also be part of a healthy relationship, and need not necessarily lead to the sexual act. Many women can get greater enjoyment out of cuddles. **Muscle and joint pain can be obstacles to sexual activity.** Gentle massage of the affected partner as a prelude to sex can help and reduce pain. Couples will also need to experiment with various sexual positions. Side by side can be a useful position, and do not be afraid of using pillows to support tender areas such as the neck or lower back. **Couples should experiment and be open in their discussion of each experiment.**

If the patient is the man, the situation is slightly easier. Some patients find it difficult to maintain an erection, but matters are helped if the woman is first well-lubricated. Again, a useful position is with the woman on top. **Both partners will need to develop great patience.** When the patient is a woman, there may be a need to consider sex differently. Most women consider quality rather than quantity. Whereas, men would usually prefer to eat bread regularly rather than starve for the feasts on good days. A solution is for the patient to masturbate the man between feasts. **In these circumstances, it is an act of giving and sharing.** It can keep a relationship alive, release tension and be enjoyable to both partners.

Sadly, in some situations sexual intercourse is not possible. Some men may develop severe prostatitis and ejaculation can be very painful. Similarly, some women can find the sex act too painful. In these situations,

93

masturbation of the partner should be seriously considered. Fortunately, these circumstances are uncommon. **Indeed, some patients find orgasm as the one activity that totally relieves their symptoms.** This is probably because of the release of adrenaline and endorphins, but unfortunately the effects are short-lived and much energy is consumed in the process. Yet, sex is important for all relationships and should have a high priority because of its great benefits.

SUMMARY

1. To understand energy, patients should think of it as money. PVFS patients need to use only the energy (money) that they have.

2. Different types of activity use more/less energy. Activities may result in symptoms days later.

3. Stress is reduced when the resources of the person are increased or the demands on the person are reduced.

4. Patients may need to lose their friends before they can get better. Relatives are usually supportive, but occasionally are too demanding.

5. The family unit can determine whether a patient recovers. The patient's role within the family will have to change and help will have to be accepted.

6. Partners have an almost impossible task. For relationships to survive, couples need to rethink their attitudes. Sexual activities are very important

and there may need to be discussion and experimentation.

Important facts

Patients must understand energy and think of it as money. Exercise, stress and relationships lose energy. Therefore patients need to understand the use of energy (money) in these situations. In particular, all of the patient's relationships need to be assessed and changes in behaviour adopted.

CHAPTER NINE

FOURTH STEP: GAINING ENERGY: SLEEP AND UNWIND

Sleep and the ability to unwind are a bit like a loyal dog – easily forgotten and conveniently left at home. Yet, to sleep and unwind are two important skills for living in the modern world. Nevertheless, many people cannot sleep; and our emphasis on physical activities can mean that many are unable to unwind. How can two natural body functions become difficult goals? The answer is simple: **many have not been taught the ability to sleep and unwind.** Both are necessary skills which take time to acquire, and much practice is required for one to become proficient. In schools of the future, they will be as important as learning how to cook. **PVFS patients need to know that sleep and the ability to unwind result in gaining energy** (Figure 16). The more energy that is gained in this way, the more energy is available for physical and mental activities. Patients need to develop these new skills as a high priority.

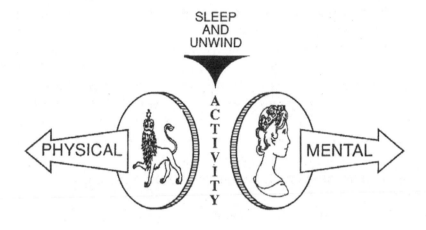

Figure 16   The ten-pence coin
Sleep and the ability to unwind earn energy. The two sides of the ten-pence coin show how money (energy) is spent. The lion represents physical activity, and the head represents mental activity.

SLEEP

Sleep has been described as the great restorer of the body. During the day, the body breaks down tissues faster than they can be renewed; whereas at night, the process of renewal is greater. There is not only physical repair of muscles, **but the brain also requires time for renewal and reorganisation of information acquired during the day.** With sleep the body is not only able to increase the rate of repair of damaged tissues, but also to reduce the rate of breakdown of normal tissues. **It is an attempt by the body to make itself better. Avoidance of sleep delays the repair of muscles.** Many patients are aware of muscle and joint pain, know that they need repair but still try and avoid "too much sleep". Patients should not be afraid of sleep, but instead help their bodies by increasing the hours of sleep.

The brain needs sleep. Brain function is more profoundly impaired by sleep deprivation than any other organ of the body. We are all aware of the tremendous reduction in brain function when we do not have enough sleep. It makes sense that the brain needs sleep as it has to remain on a "red alert" state during the whole day. Thus, a period of repair of the brain circuits and reassessment of the day's events is essential before the next day. **Sleep is curative.** It is summarised by Shakespeare's words in Macbeth:

"Sleep that knits up the ravell'd sleave of care,
The death of each day's life, sore labour's bath,
Balm of hurt minds, great nature's second course,
Chief nourisher in life's feast."

98

1. Sleep Fallacies

Fallacies are incorrect, inaccurate or misleading facts. This is particularly true about facts on sleep. The public perceives good sleep to be: instant sleep as soon as the head touches the pillow; total unconsciousness for eight hours; no vivid dreams; and awakening totally refreshed. **This perception of sleep is too simple and is inaccurate in many ways.** For PVFS patients, they need to learn the truth about sleep and get rid of many of their fallacies. As sleep is so important, some popular incorrect facts must be carefully considered:

a) Awakening during the night

It is considered to be very poor sleep if one wakes during the night. It is not recognised that this concept of sleep has been learnt: babies do not sleep through the night, and in terms of survival it makes more sense to wake frequently. Sleeping throughout the night is learned behaviour designed for modern living; and with illness, there is often a reversion to a more natural sleeping pattern with frequent awakening.

b) Length of sleep

Most people need an average of 8 hours sleep per night. With the 24/7 society, many people have a chronic sleep deficit, and some are surviving on 4 hours sleep a day. However, there are great differences with age: a baby of two months sleeps 18 hours, a three-year old for 13 hours, a twenty-five year old for 8 hours and a seventy-five year old for 5 hours. In addition, **centuries ago, people were able to vary their sleeping hours with the seasons of the year.** Thus in winter, they would sleep 14-16 hours and thus have less need for food, warmth or light. Whilst in the summer, they would sleep 4-6 hours and make use of the daylight. Today, how many can do this?   Indeed, **many patients wrongly believe that more than 8 hours sleep per night is "abnormal"!**

A constant complaint of patients is the increased amount of sleep that they require. For some, double the sleeping time still does not seem to be enough. Others try to stop themselves sleeping as they fear "sleeping their lives away". It is important to realise that there is a reason for sleep: their bodies are trying to repair damage. **Sleep, unlike fat, is not stored in the body.**   The analogy with fat is instructive. For many patients their only experience of being responsible for their own health is in the control of their weight. To remove fat one stops eating. Thus, it seems logical if one sleeps too much, to stop sleeping. **But, one sleeps to recover from the past and not to prepare for the future.** Restrictions on sleep can make matters worse. **A catastrophic double mistake is if a patient decides to "snap" out of his condition by excessive exercise and reduced sleep.** This is like getting a £10,000 loan to repay a debt, burning the money and wondering why there is no improvement in the financial position.

c) Vivid dreams
Everyone dreams every night.   Many people do not realise that they need to dream every night. If dreaming is prevented by **awakening individuals as they start to dream, severe psychological symptoms can develop.** In some societies, talking and remembering dreams are an important part of the day. However, in the West, we have been taught to forget our dreams. When faced with a child having had a vivid dream, parents often say: "forget the dream and go to sleep". Or: "it was only a

100

dream, think of something else". This teaches the child that dreams are not important and should be forgotten. **In PVFS, vivid dreams are common and are normal and should not be a source of worry.**

d) Terrible sleep

If patients do not understand sleep cycles, they frequently complain of terrible sleep. There are natural cycles at 20-30 minutes and at 90 minutes. If patients awake at these times, they feel refreshed. However, if patients awake at 60 minutes, they may be in the deepest stage of sleep. This is when a sleeper is "dead to the world" and ignores outside stimulation such as a telephone ringing. If patients awake at this stage, **they feel terrible and not refreshed so many become convinced that sleep makes them worse.** There is much that patients need to learn about sleep.

e) Night into day

Very many patients get into the habit of getting up late, watching too much television and going to bed late. They end up sleeping during the day and staying up all night. **This is a similar position to individuals who have jet-lag or are working a night shift.** It is perhaps complicated by the natural biological clock which works a 25-hour day, so there is a natural inclination to turn night into day. This inclination has to be corrected by frequent adjustments to our 24-hour day such as work, radio, television, etc. Re-adjusting the body clock back to normal is not easy. **The answer is that patients have to go to bed 3 hours later each "night" and get up 3 hours later each "morning".** After a few days, patients can go to bed and get up at a chosen time. They must now stick to this new schedule. Any late nights and they will have to repeat the treatment all over again.

2. Insomnia

Many patients have difficulty sleeping because of several common problems:

a) Symptoms. A host of symptoms can easily interfere with a good night's sleep. Hotness or coldness, twitching muscles, muscle cramps, muscle and joint pains, itching and numbness of arms or legs are common complaints. With all of these symptoms, it **is important not to become annoyed or angry with being woken up.** It is best to adopt an attitude of being woken up by a mischievous child or pet, and try to get back to sleep. Leg muscle cramps are worrying, but pulling the toes towards the shin is usually effective. If you do this several times before you go to sleep, it may prevent cramps developing.

b) Active mind. An active mind which is unable to switch off and go to sleep is commonly found. Many patients complain that they feel physically exhausted but cannot stop their mind thinking and worrying. **It is critical that patients develop the ability to blank their minds.** It is best to do an "unwind exercise". This is very important and is considered in more detail in the "Unwind" section of this chapter.

c) Early awakening. Another common complaint is to wake after a few hours sleep and not be able to go back to sleep. **A quick return to sleep depends on an adoption of an unwind exercise and not doing more thinking.** The most common mistake is to start thinking and become worried, anxious and wide awake. When this happens, it can help to get out of bed, have a drink of water and then return to bed and go through an unwind exercise. A few patients have **early morning awakening.** This is often when patients are agitated or anxious. It might be accompanied by depression. The best remedy is to deal with the anxiety or depression, and then sleep will return to normal.

3. Aids to sleep
Getting to sleep is not a lottery. There are many things that you can do to increase your sleep success:

a) Regular sleeping times. A good routine produces good sleep. If you go to bed and awaken at the same time each day, good sleep is usually certain.

b) Beds and pillows. A good night's sleep is dependent on good equipment. A firm bed can be the difference between having a good night's sleep and not. Pillows are very useful especially if you have painful areas, for example if you sleep on your side it can be useful to have a pillow between your knees. You may need to experiment to find the right type of pillow. Bed linen is also important and natural fabrics are the most comfortable.

c) Light, noise, temperature. It is more difficult to sleep in a well-lit room. Darkness is best and an investment in well-lined curtains can be a great help. Some patients find it easier if they wear sleeping patches over their eyes. Whereas some individuals are able to sleep through noise, most people find external noise distracts them from sleeping. The use of earplugs can help. The temperature is a critical factor and a bedroom should be around 16^{0}C. The body becomes coldest at around 4am in the morning so in the winter the heating should be set to come on in the early morning.

d) Anger and anxieties. Very few people can go to bed angry and sleep easily. Most find themselves thinking about the problem. If you have difficulties turning your mind off, unwind sessions can help. Similarly, if you are angry, it is best to write down your feelings on a piece of paper and promise yourself to deal with the matter the next morning. Finally, a good scream or punching a pillow can be a great release.

e) Food and Drinks. Eating a large meal close to bedtime does not help sleep. Certain foods, such as cheese can be particularly incompatible with good sleep. It is not a good idea to drink tea, coffee or alcohol just before bedtime. These are stimulants and keep you awake. Nevertheless, malted, milky drinks (such as Horlicks or Ovaltine) help sleep.

f) Prepare for sleeping. This means that you should not be watching emotional television, listening to stimulating music or playing computer games before going to bed. Worse, do not have a very emotional argument before bed. It is best to read a book or have a hot bath.

4. Naps
There is a range of opinion on naps or short sleeps. Many feel that only the lazy members of society need to take naps, and the strong do not need such time-outs.

There is also the image of the overweight Pickwickian character who eats and sleeps all of the time. Another strong image is of elderly people who are always falling asleep in front of the television or when there are visitors. There is no doubt that in Britain **naps are assigned to the lazy, overweight or elderly.**

In southern Europe, the position is quite different. **The siesta is part of the life-style and culture.** These naps after lunch reflect the sleepiness after eating and the hot midday temperatures. However, a great advantage is that it allows individuals to stay up later at night. Many feel that **the body's natural internal sleep-wake clock is designed for two sleeps a day** (a short one in the afternoon and a long one at night). Many patients who are unaccustomed to naps can find them daunting. A feeling of being a zombie after a nap is usually due to the individual getting up in the wrong part of the sleep cycle. In addition, **it takes time to learn to nap** and patients often do not feel real benefit until 2-3 months later. Like all great skills, much effort is required for one to become proficient.

Another common argument against naps is that if there is sleep during the day, the person would not be able to sleep at night. Again there is some truth in this, but there is also some benefit. In PVFS patients, the total sleep for a 24-hour period has to be increased, so if one slept during the day, there is a smaller requirement in the night sleep. However, it also **takes time to adjust to two sleeps per day.** Among high-achieving managers, the concept of the "power-nap" has evolved. This short 20-30 minute sleep is now the norm in many companies. Very many great world leaders have been addicted to naps. Winston Churchill and Margaret Thatcher are two excellent examples. The message is clear: **when you have very little time for sleep, naps are a great bonus.** It is a valuable lesson to PVFS patients. Naps gain time and energy.

UNWIND

In the modern world, people have to be "keyed up" and "ready to go". It is therefore not surprising that many people are "wound up" at the end of the day. These people need to "unwind" as a full life involves movement between these two states: **a person needs to be wound up at certain times and unwound** at others. Sadly, whilst most people are able to wind themselves up, only a minority are able to unwind. **Many PVFS patients need to learn to unwind.** Why have I chosen to use the word **"unwind"** instead of **"relaxation"**? Both of these words have similar meanings, however, there are important differences.

Firstly, relaxation is usually more associated with muscles, for example "make less rigid", whereas I am more concerned with the relaxation of the mind. Secondly, relaxation is often associated with "recreation". Although the concept of re-creating (or making again") is consistent with my views, other interpretations of recreation (such as "interval of free time") are not the objectives that I have. **Lastly, "unwind" epitomises my approach of "undoing", "unravelling" or "disentangling" life's problems.** Relaxation is often used to mean "not being active", "sitting in front of the television", "resting", or "recreation". Many patients think that this can do them good. Indeed they quickly remind others how this compared with their previous energetic activities. Unfortunately, sitting in front of a television rarely does PVFS patients a lot of good. **To unwind is an active process which creates energy and allows patients to recharge their batteries.**

A special unwind technique, **EMBME**, has been developed for PVFS patients. This technique is described in detail ("Unwind! Understand and control life, be better!!" by Dr Darrel Ho-Yen, Dodona Books, 1991 ISBN 0-9511090-0-2-2). Patients continue to find this book valuable as it greatly aids recovery.
The unwind technique has five stages:

a)   **Entrance:** requires that enough time should be set aside, there should be mental commitment, a quiet comfortable place and enough concentration.

b)   **Muscles:** With the patient lying down or sitting in a comfortable chair, there is sequential, gradual contraction and relaxation of the muscles in the legs, abdomen, arms, shoulders and face.

c)   **Breathing:** Breathe in fully and breathe out fully. Repeat this three times and then breathe naturally and softly. Count up to fifty and then proceed to the next stage.

d)   **Mind control:** This stage unwinds the mind by concentrating on a peaceful scene (such as a tree, beach, lake or mountain) in your imagination with your eyes closed. Remove any unwanted thoughts. Repetition of the word EMBME again and again can help.

e) **Exit:** Open your eyes slowly, appreciate your surroundings and yawn. Stretch arms and legs. Slowly get up. Shout "EMBME!"

Best results from unwinding are obtained when an individual has two half hour sessions each day. At times of stress, there should be four sessions per day. **Remember that it takes time to learn to unwind.** Most people take several months before there is great benefit, but then there can be immediate boosts to their energy levels.

DAILY DIARY

Sleep and unwind sessions are two very important parts of the daily diary. Patients should **record the total number of hours in a 24-hour day that they are lying down in bed with their eyes closed and with no noise in the room.** I do not mind if patients are not asleep.

However, it is critical that there is no noise in the room. It is also important that patients try and not to think or worry. If sleep is taken in several periods during the day, record only **the total amount for the day.** The diary of patients who are still at work frequently shows a pattern of 6-7 hours sleep from Monday to Friday, and 11-12 hours sleep on Saturday/Sunday. Obviously **patients are suffering from sleep deficit during the week and making up for this at weekends.** The way forward is to agree that the minimum sleep each night from Monday to Friday is 7 hours, and the minimum for Saturday/Sunday is 12 hours. **This simple change can produce dramatic changes in scores.**

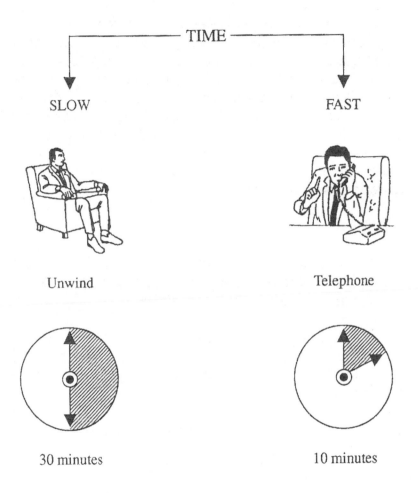

Figure 17   Time: slow and fast
Time goes slowly when patients have an unwind session.
Thirty minutes can appear to be 1 hour. However, time goes
fast when patients are on the telephone; and one hour can
appear to be ten minutes.

Unwind sessions are very important and each session should be recorded, e.g. unwind x 2. Ideally, **a patient should have at least two sessions per day.** As this is a means of gaining extra energy, it is particularly useful before periods of increased demands, for example on the day before a night out. It is better before the event than after. Time goes slowly when patients are having an unwind session (Figure 17). This is because many are bored. However, when on the telephone, patients are stimulated and time goes fast. Patients prefer to be on the telephone but an unwind session is more beneficial. **Boredom saves energy.**

SUMMARY

1. PVFS patients need to learn to sleep and unwind to gain energy. Sleep is necessary for muscle and brain renewal. Sleep is curative.

2. There are many sleep myths but PVFS patients must learn the truth. Insomnia is caused by many factors and patients should take appropriate actions.

3. There are many aids to sleep. In addition, naps allow people to be refreshed during the day and reduce the overall requirement for sleep.

4. The ability to unwind must be learnt. The technique EMBME is a major skill which aids recovery.

5.   The daily diary must include total hours a patient is in bed with their eyes closed with no noise in the room.   Unwind sessions should be carried out at least twice daily and the number recorded.

Important Facts

Patients must understand sleep. Ideally, they should learn how to get better sleep and to nap. Recovery is faster in patients who have learnt to sleep and unwind.

CHAPTER TEN
FIFTH STEP:
MAKING ENERGY LAST

To make energy last is very hard work. **Very many PVFS patients do not want to work at making energy last.** To many onlookers, it seems an easy solution to their problem. However, for patients, it will take some time before they consider the great benefits of making energy last. **Instead, they are happier to ask, beg and cry for good health.** If patients would like to **work** at making energy last, there are simple rules: use less; be more efficient; and be joyful. Although these rules are simple, **for PVFS patients they are extremely difficult as this involves facing the truth of their situation and taking appropriate action.** Like much of life, it can be easier to deceive oneself than face the truth.

Two good examples from life may also help. When people lose their job, it can be a long time before they adjust to their reduced circumstances. Instead, they continue to spend money as before, hoping to be employed soon. **The position is similar to PVFS**

patients, and as with unemployment, those individuals who adjust best, do so early. Patients need to live within their reduced budget (energy and money) today. **Another example emphasises the need to develop skills.** If one gave a group of people £10 each to spend on food for a week, there would be a variety of results. Some would not be able to feed themselves for one day as they buy food ready-made. Others would be able to eat for two weeks as they have cooking skills. PVFS patients have to learn the skills of making money (energy) last.

USE LESS

It is fairly obvious if you use less energy, you will have more left. However, I am frequently asked: "How can I do with less? I am struggling to get through the day with what I have!" Over the years, I have developed several approaches to help patients in these situations.

1. Go slow
I once had a teacher who went through life at three speeds: slow, dead slow and stop. Everyone ridiculed him. Yet, he was one of the most well-adjusted individuals that I have known. He recognised that **rushing around is a great waste of energy.** I am always saddened when I walk down a corridor with a patient and the patient is walking faster than I. It is as though he/she has something to prove. Patients are ill so why do they want to walk faster? Some hospitals insist that patients should be in wheelchairs. It is sensible. So, **why do some patients hate the suggestion that they should use a wheelchair?** To me, it seems sensible that if you do not have a lot of energy, you do not spend

what you have in walking. Worse, to try and walk faster than normal people seems to be particularly stupid. Also, **how can people believe that you are ill if you behave this way?** Again and again, PVFS patients must recognise that they will be treated by the general public as they behave. **It is just to be judged by your actions.**

2. Never do two things at once

An American President was once described as someone who could not chew gum and walk at the same time. It was a tremendous joke and produced much hilarity. No one bothered to consider how someone who was an American President could achieve so much whilst being so incapable. For PVFS patients, **it makes great sense never to do two things at once.** Working people have breakfast, read the papers and listen to the radio or television at the same time, all in 30 minutes. This uses up a lot of energy **as it requires a lot of concentration. For PVFS patients, these should be separate activities.** Thus, patients should have breakfast (30 minutes), make coffee and drink it slowly (30 minutes), read the papers (30 minutes) and then listen to the radio or television (30 minutes). **What previously took 30 minutes should now take 2 hours; it uses less energy and makes available resources last.** Also, 1½ hours have been used and the time can be enjoyed.

BE MORE EFFICIENT

To many, being more efficient means that you accomplish more. Before they were ill, many PVFS patients could do more in a day than those around them. However, as a patient, to be more efficient is not

114

measured in accomplishment but in how exhausted you are. **The test is to go to bed with money (energy) unspent.** The rules have changed. If you do not play according to the new rules, you will not get better.

1. Boredom periods

"To bore" means "to tire by being dull, repetitious or uninteresting". It is what most PVFS patients detest – the last thing that they would want to do. Over the last few years, the **greatest change in my management technique is to recommend boredom periods.** Why? Because if one is bored, then one is using less energy. When we are stimulated and excited, adrenaline flows and we use maximum energy. Is it not better to be bored and wanting to go to sleep? Most patients answer this question by saying that if they were bored all day, they would become depressed.... and that would be even worse! I agree. So the answer is to have **both boredom and excitement, and also lose less energy.** How can this be achieved?

It can be achieved by breaking the day up into half hour periods (Figure 18). For example, if you would like to watch television, precede this period with a boredom period and after the half-hour of television have another boredom period. **Whilst you are being bored, try and look forward to your indulgence – a period of television.** In this way, you will probably find that you will enjoy the television even more than normal. The end result is you have **paid** for the period of television **and** you have enjoyed it more. This compares with individuals sitting in front of the television all day getting more and more tired, and not enjoying anything they see.

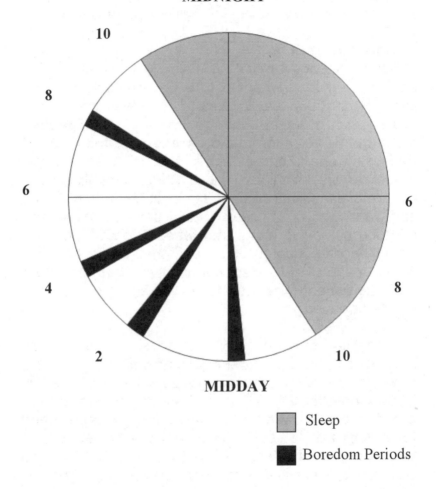

Figure 18   The perfect day
The ideal day is broken up into many half-hour slots, with lots of boredom periods. It takes practice before this timetable can be perfected.   However, it can allow you to enjoy your activities more <u>and</u> be rested.

What do you do in boredom periods? I like simple things: watching clouds in the sky, trees in the wood, fish in a fish tank, and rain running down a window. **When you become expert at boredom periods, you can watch grass grow.** This is when you know that you have become professional at making energy last. It will not be easy. You will detest yourself every moment that you do it. **Yet, it will make you better!** At least two half-hour periods each day are recommended, but four such periods are best.

2. Save little bits

Do you know anyone who saves left-over pennies or small coins? Many individuals have a bottle in which they put these savings. My sons like to build great piles of pennies and two-pence pieces. It is an annoying habit. But, in time, there is usually several pounds worth of savings. **PVFS patients have to be misers with their energy and take every opportunity to save a little bit** (Figure 19). Healthy individuals can be carefree in how they spend their energy. When there is plenty, there is no need for a strategy. **When there is little energy, a strategy is essential.** How do you save? It depends on adopting a different mental attitude. Instead of trying to finish the gardening, you stop early when the job is half done. You plan to stay two hours at the party, but leave 10 minutes early. You plan to go shopping for one hour, but come home after 50 minutes. If you say someone can visit for an hour and they stay longer, you insist that they leave after an hour and five minutes; usually patients allow them to stay for 2 hours. **Every little bit of energy that is saved is there for tomorrow.** More importantly, it means that you do not have to borrow energy today. If you do not have to go into your reserves

Figure 19 Big spender and miser
Healthy individuals are big spenders and can throw away
pound notes. Whereas PVFS patients must be misers with
their money (energy), and count every penny. This can be a
major change of lifestyle for some patients.

it means that your body has more energy to heal itself now. **If the body can start to heal itself now, it is obvious that you will get better faster.** It simply makes sense.

BE JOYFUL

Joy is defined as a deep feeling of happiness and contentment. With many patients this does not happen often. Yet, **for all of us, there will be something in every day that is good.** It may be a song, a joke, an odd occurrence or even some sunshine in an overcast day. To make energy last, PVFS patients have to be joyful at these times.

1. Good activities

All activities do not use the same amount of energy. Patients should learn to identify good activities. The golden rule is to ask yourself if you are bored with the activity. If you are not bored but you are interested, then the activity is likely to use up a lot of energy and is a bad activity. **So, it is best to listen to music that you do not like, you will not be as involved and less energy will be used.** Classical, operatic or ethnic music is better than songs with words and emotion. **Care should be made in the selection of television programmes or videos.** If a programme has too much action or emotion, patients adopt the actors' roles and use as much adrenaline as the actors. Love stories and drama are very effective at using up energy. Good programmes are on nature, travel or cooking as they use up very little energy. Indeed, two hours of a cooking programme uses as much energy as half an hour of an emotional, daily soap programme. **A good idea is to decide on the type**

of programme based on your scores. Activities such as watching fish in a fish tank or a pet playing with itself are good at making energy last. Although pets can be a great help to recovery, large dogs that need daily exercise are not. **The cat which looks after itself is a much better role model for a patient.** Indeed, if patients can adopt the single-mindedness of a cat, recovery is assured.

2. Good scores
When you get a good score in your diary, it should be enjoyed. Like receiving a prize, **one should take some time to enjoy the moment. Patients should also enjoy the feel of the score.** Scores are not what you can do, **but what you feel that you can do.** Sadly, some patients have a negative response to a good score. There is disbelief followed by the thought that the score is only true if the individual could do more. They then try to do activities representing the score. When there is the predictable relapse, the patient's retort is that it shows that the score was not real. **It is a powerful self-fulfilling prophecy.** The daily diary is not only a source of information but also encouragement. The low scores give warning that there is too much activity. The high scores are rewards for good practice. As the high scores have been hard won, **they should be treasured.** Then, high scores can produce more high scores and success follows. A very good reason to be joyful.

SUMMARY

1.   Patients have to be prepared to work at making energy last. Much has to be learnt and put into practice.

2. Patients must use less energy. They must slow their lives down. Their ability to do this will aid recovery but also make others recognise that they are ill.

3. Patients must use energy more efficiently. There should be boredom periods (at least 2) every day.

4. Patients have to be misers with their energy, and take every opportunity to save a little bit of energy.

5. Patients must be joyful. They need to recognise good activities and avoid bad activities.

6. Good scores should be treasured and enjoyed. They represent rewards for good practice.

Important facts

It is very difficult to make energy (money) last. Patients have to learn strategies to use less, become efficient and save more. Once learnt, these skills can bring great joy.

CHAPTER ELEVEN
FOOD

For PVFS patients, food is vitally important for recovery. **With illness, food is required for healing.** It is important for all ill patients to have sufficient protein (meat, chicken, fish), carbohydrates (bread, rice), vitamins and minerals (vegetables and fruits). Vegetarians must particularly make sure that **they are eating sufficient protein.** Fortunately, most patients living as part of a family are likely to eat well. For the vast majority of patients, deficiencies in the food consumed does not happen. Problems are likely to occur when patients live alone because there is the temptation to miss meals. Patients often say that they are not hungry and have no energy to cook. After some weeks, the less you eat, the less you want to eat. **If a patient is not eating normally then major problems may arise,** including anorexia nervosa. Sadly, this is becoming more and more common among young women patients.

Most patients do not require extra vitamins and much money can be saved. Only patients who are not eating normally may benefit from extra vitamins. There has been a concern that PVFS patients can be deficient in minerals (iron, zinc, etc), but this is very, very rare.

PUTTING ON WEIGHT

This can be a major worry. Before their illness, many patients were very active with great appetites. With illness, **patients have become inactive but still have continued to eat**, and so have put on weight. Normally weight loss is achieved by combining exercise and reduced food intake. For PVFS patients, there is not the option of exercise. Therefore food intake has to be significantly reduced. **For patients in their first year of illness, I do not recommend dieting**. Instead, they should focus on understanding energy. Once they get better, there will be enough time to lose weight and get fit again. **Some patients find it impossible to eat less.** For these patients, it can be easier to substitute foods. Obviously if you can substitute carrots/celery for your snacks of chocolate or ice-cream, **there are less calories but the same volume**.

FOOD CAUSES PVFS

After a viral infection, patients may develop food allergies which can result in severe and worrying symptoms. The vast majority of PVFS patients do **not** have food allergies. **Food allergy is the immediate reaction to tiny amounts of a specific food.** It is often a life-long problem and total avoidance of the specific food is the main treatment. **Food allergies can produce similar complaints to those of PVFS.** This is not surprising as both may be caused by abnormalities in the immune system. The situation is further complicated as PVFS patients can develop food allergies, and symptoms may be due to either. Fortunately, it is possible to separate the two conditions by testing for food allergies. **If symptoms are due to food allergies, they will go away when the causative food is not eaten.** If symptoms are due to PVFS, they will **not** go away with a change of diet. Instead, only the slow recovery from the viral infection will see the disappearance of the complaints.

1. Self-testing
The simplest method of testing is the exclusion diet. Over a period of weeks, various foods are introduced into the diet and their effects observed. If there is no adverse effect, the food is excluded as a possible cause of the symptom. Ideally, the patient should start with a **5-day fast**, however, as this is very difficult for working people, it is more appropriate for those being tested in hospital. **An alternative start is to eat pork (or fish) for 3 meals a day for 5 days.** During this time no other food is eaten. As much spring water (bottled Malvern water) as desired can be drunk, but tap water is avoided (because of impurities, especially chlorine).

After the 5 days, a suspected food is eaten by itself instead of the evening meal (if a drink is to be tested, it is drunk after the usual meal of pork or fish). **If the food is causing an allergy, symptoms return within a few hours.** In this way, different foods and drink are slowly incriminated or excluded. Records must be detailed and all food taken every day must be recorded. If one particular food produces a severe reaction, the testing should not stop as a patient may be allergic to more than one food or group of foods.

Severe reactions may be stopped by drinking a tablespoon of sodium bicarbonate (bicarbonate of soda) in a half-pint of warm water. The sodium bicarbonate produces diarrhoea and so gets rid of the offending food. The theory behind starting with 5 days of meat (Cave Man diet) is that man has been eating meat for thousands of years and it is thus less likely to cause allergy. Whereas, only much later did man start to eat cereals and sugars and so these are more likely to cause allergy. The end result of testing is that patients should know if they have a food allergy. **No improvement during the 5-day fast or the 5-day diet of pork implies that there is no food allergy.** At the end of testing, if there is food allergy, there is a list of foods that produce symptoms. These foods can be confirmed as a cause of problems by **"challenging"**. This is the introduction of the food at a later date to see if symptoms are still produced. Some patients find, after several months, **that they are able to eat a particular food without side-effects when previously the same food produced symptoms.** Thus patients may need to rotate foods to adjust to symptoms developing or going away.

2. Hospital testing

Hospital testing is more complete, but unfortunately there are few of these specialised units. Patients are starved for 5-days, but during this time they can drink as much spring water as they want. **If there is no improvement after the 5 days, the patient does not have a food allergy.** Improvement in symptoms suggest food allergy and the patient is then tested with one new food a day. In hospitals, other tests such as skin tests or testing of blood for particular IgE antibodies can also be performed. **These IgE antibodies (RAST) tests are available in**

most District General Hospital laboratories. There is national, external quality assurance for these tests; and, if local hospitals cannot do the tests, it can be sent to another hospital for testing. These test results are reproducible in hospital laboratories throughout Britain.

3. Commercial Allergy Testing

Facilities for testing for allergies in the National Health Service are limited. This has resulted in an increase in commercial allergy testing. It is easy to find adverts offering allergy testing on hair samples or blood. The information on the test appears dependable but expensive. If you got tested, you would get back several pages of results on many foods. **Unfortunately, these laboratories perform very poorly when tested.** When the laboratory was sent two samples from the same patient, the results that came back were different. Also, the laboratory reported allergies that did not exist. The truth is that these tests are not dependable.

4. Pseudo-Food Allergy

This is when the patient has an underlying psychological problem rather than a food allergy[13]. **The patient focuses on food allergy as the solution to his problems.** There is an immediate placebo benefit from the exclusion of a particular food. However, it does not last. To maintain improvement, there has to be continual placebo benefits from continual exclusion of foods. As this continues, there can be a serious risk of malnutrition and severe anorexia.

5. Food Intolerance

Food intolerance requires **large quantities of the offending food and symptoms occur many hours**

126

later. The usual skin tests and laboratory tests which are used to diagnose food allergy are negative with food intolerance. **Diagnosis of food intolerance depends on developing symptoms when exposed to the offending food.** Patients should start with an exclusion diet as in excluding food allergy. Unlike food allergy, the reaction in food intolerance can be delayed and occur the next day. However, similar to food allergy, if symptoms do not improve on a 5 day diet of pork or fish, food intolerance is unlikely. **Food intolerance in PVFS patients may be more common than food allergy.** Patients who are recently ill without abdominal complaints are unlikely to have food allergy or intolerance.

ABNORMAL RESPONSE TO FOOD

With illness, there can be abnormal responses to food.

1. Illness/age
As individuals become older, the body slows down. In some people, abdominal complaints such as pain, feeling of being bloated or uncomfortable can become frequent. These individuals do not have food allergies or intolerance. **PVFS patients can have these symptoms accentuated.** Again, with illness, one can see that the gastrointestinal tract may not function as efficiently as in good health. Whatever the cause of these abdominal complaints, my recommendation is the **Hay System** (discussed later). Probiotics may also relieve symptoms and are worth trying.

2. Alcohol

Alcohol intolerance is common in PVFS patients and may affect up to 30% of patients. Alcohol can adversely affect PVFS patients in at least two ways. It may be part of a food allergy, alternatively it may be the direct action of alcohol. Surprisingly, it is not excessive alcohol intake (PVFS patients are rarely alcoholic), but moderate amounts that can have profound effects. **Many patients have profound tiredness and exhaustion after alcohol.**

DIETS

Concern about food and dieting is usually to lose weight. For patients with severe abdominal complaints or illness for many years, they diet to feel better. Sadly, there are many available diets, and some of these diets require large amounts of time (Figure 20). **If you cannot find the time and energy to eat normally, you do not have sufficient time or energy for a diet.** The **anti-candida** diets have many advocates, but are time-consuming and can be quite expensive. I do **not** feel that most patients benefit from this diet. **I would rather patients take the time and effort to understand energy.**

The diet that I have found most helpful to patients is the **"Hay System".** This is superbly explained in: "Food Combining for Health" by Doris Grant and Jean Joice (2004, Thorsons). There are five major rules:

a)   starches and sugars should not be eaten with proteins and acid fruits at the same meal.

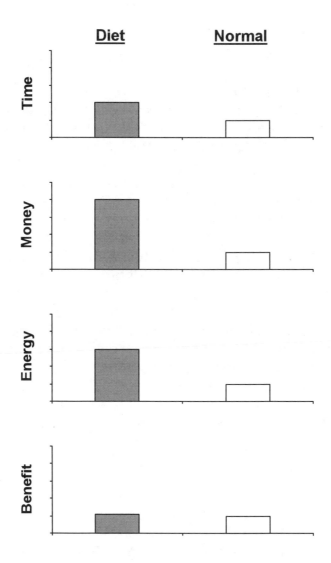

Figure 20.   Costs of diets
Diets take up a lot of time (x2); a great deal of money (x4); and
a lot of energy (x3).   Most patients do not benefit.   Some get a
small benefit.

b)   vegetables, salads and fruits are the major part of the diet.
c)   proteins, starches and fats should be eaten in small quantities.
d)   refined, processed foods should be avoided.
e)   an interval of 4-5 hours should elapse between meals of different character.

How does the Hay System benefit PVFS patients? Complete answers are not available. However, in patients with severe abdominal complaints or long illness, it is likely that the gastrointestinal tract is affected with disease. **The Hay System reduces the workload for a patient with gastrointestinal dysfunction.** Whereas an unaffected gastrointestinal tract can easily cope with whatever is ingested, it makes sense to combine foods with similar digestive requirements when there is abnormal function of the gastrointestinal tract. **Small, more frequent meals and eating the major meal in the middle of the day can be helpful.** Patients who have been ill under one year should not worry about diets; **this cannot be emphasised too much.**

SUMMARY

1.   PVFS patients require a healthy diet as food is required for healing the body.

2.   Lots of patients put on weight. Patients should not worry about this, but focus on getting better.

3.   Food allergies can cause similar symptoms to PVFS. Very few patients have food allergies.

4. Patients do not have a food allergy or intolerance if they are not better after 5 days of fasting or 5 days of a pork (or fish) diet.

5. Patients can have abnormal responses to food and drink, especially alcohol.

6. The diet that is the most successful is the Hay System and this can be tried before food testing.

Important facts

Patients need good food to heal and recover. They should not worry about putting on weight. Food allergies are uncommon. Abdominal complaints are best dealt with by the use of probiotics or the Hay System.

CHAPTER TWELVE
EMPLOYMENT

Apart from its social status, employment has great psychological effects. With work, individuals feel that they are contributing to the community. They feel useful. They are playing their part. There is a sense of belonging, income, social contacts and purpose. It is a team game and these people are good to have on your team. Suddenly, with PVFS, their role has been changed. **Instead of a valuable member of the team, there is a handicapped one.** Others have to do more work. The patient feels guilty. Not only is self-esteem lost, but also there is the realisation that they are helped, tolerated, even patronised. Illness is compounded by guilt and self-criticism. **Many feel that they are given a gun, and asked to do the honourable thing – shoot themselves.**

There is an excellent editorial in the British Medical Journal[14] entitled: **"Without work all life goes rotten."** Its message is clear: unemployment kills, ruins health and destroys families. It is not certain how unemployment kills, but it is probably a combination of the adoption of unhealthy behaviour, poverty, stress and a poor mental attitude to life. All can seem hopeless. **Yet, patients should remember that life has good bits and bad bits.** Illness is a bad bit. If you cannot cope with the bad bits of life, you have not learnt about life. With illness, you have to concentrate on **the major test of life which is not work, but survival.** Patients must remember that to survive and get better is the ultimate test.

FULL-TIME EMPLOYMENT

Ideally, individuals should enjoy their work and their work should influence their health (Figure 21). As this figure shows, **many PVFS patients find themselves in the position where work results in a worsening of their health.** This is often because they are working inefficiently, and using a large amount of energy to achieve a mediocre result. Before they became unwell, they were able to do a job in 1 hour; with illness the same job may take 4 hours and have mistakes.

1. Keeping a job.
Most PVFS patients would have taken only a few days off work with their initial illness. Some would have taken no time off work. Going back to work is a test of "moral fibre"; those with low moral fibre have to have sick leave. Not only should there be an early return to work, "high achievers" make up for the time off when they return. In this way, **the patient is quickly exhausted and then the real problems begin.** The diagnosis of PVFS should not be made until the patient has been ill for 3 months. Fatigue for 2-3 months may rarely complicate many viral illnesses. Using a 3-month cut-off point is arbitrary, but

133

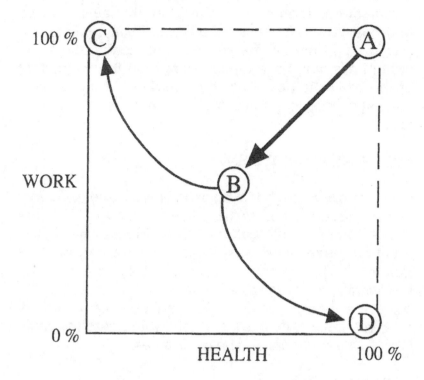

Figure 21   Work and health
At position A, full-time work has benefits on health. As work or
health declines, the other is also reduced (B).   From this
position, some patients find that increasing work further
reduces their health (C).   Others find that part-time work or
unemployment allows their health to recover (D).

it can be useful in separating those individuals who may take longer to recover

After 3 months of being back at work, there is a predictable scenario. The patient is falling behind at work and sleeping a lot at home. **He is feeling unwell almost all of the time. There is difficulty concentrating. Bad decisions are being made.** He is a topic of conversation. The patient has a few days off, and then a few more. There may be diarrhoea, blamed on the "take-away", and some more days are taken off work. He has become a regular visitor to his doctor. There are arguments with family and friends. **What can be done?**

At this stage, a patient has to answer a number of crucial questions. **How important is work to me? What would I do if I became unemployed? How would I feel?** This is a time for deciding on priorities. The most common mistake is for the patient to try and do everything. It cannot be done. Accustomed to having £10.00 to spend on treats per day, there is now 10 pence and it has to last the whole week. **Patients cannot believe that life could have become bad so quickly.** There is a reluctance or an inability to see the situation objectively. They wake every morning, with the hope of a miracle cure overnight.

If patients want to remain employed, they have to be a miser with their energy. They have to:

a)   stop unnecessary mental and physical exertion; if the job is physical, change the job.

b)   minimise all walking. **Walk slowly always.**

135

c)   think before any physical activity.   Use the telephone, send an email.
d)   at lunchtime, unwind or have a nap.
e)   have a relaxation session or sleep as soon as you return home from work.
f)   stop all social engagements.

All of the above seem excessive. It is. It has to be. PVFS patients who want to keep their job are asking a lot – there is nothing left over for anything else. If they want to do something else, they should give up the job. If all of the above are done, then there is a **95% chance of keeping the job.** Most do not do all of the above. Most get away without losing their jobs. Most do not realise that all that they are doing is reducing their 95% chance to 70%, 50%, 30%, 10%....

Less time spent on social activities can also leave the brain free to concentrate on the job and home. Some have found that this honing down on the important things has produced more satisfaction at work and at home. At the start of the illness, both the brain and the muscles are easily exhausted. Brain function returns first and so it is possible to think normally after 2-3 months, provided that the patient is not too tired. **Indeed, a state where thinking compensates for activity, can produce better results.** Some have found promotion at work, purely because they use their time and energy more efficiently.

2. Sick leave
As many patients get a great benefit from a weekend or annual leave, **there is great optimism that a few weeks sick leave would allow them to recover.** Indeed, some

patients would be willing to make a large bet that 6 weeks of rest would result in full recovery. **It does not happen.** The more usual pattern is that there is some benefit for the first two weeks, less benefit in the second two weeks and then anxiety and concern because of the lack of recovery in the last two weeks.

When a patient has a score of 4 or 5 out of 10 it is easier for a patient to stay at work than to benefit from sick leave. I believe that this is because PVFS patients are usually individuals who derive great satisfaction from work. Work is also normal and what they are accustomed to, whereas it takes some time to adjust to sick leave. If patients feel that they need to have sick leave, **they should plan for at least three months. In many cases, it is 6-9 months.** This is because there is great adrenaline which keeps individuals at work. When this stops, it takes the first month to adjust. There is benefit in the second month which can be consolidated in the last month. **A common trap is to substitute mental or social activities for work.** Patients who are not ready to return to work after six months have a major problem. This problem is that they have been unable to stay within their energy limits.

They are unable to say "No!" to their friends and relatives, and are not in control of their lives. They do not have an understanding of energy. It can be depressing to see how patients misuse sick leave without realising what they are doing. After the first six months of full pay, the next six months of half pay are a patient's last good chance of returning to work. **Matters are now desperate, but many patients fail to recognise their situation.** Somehow there appears to be great optimism, and the failures over the previous six months are not recognised. At this stage, it is possible for patients to return to work, but **they must** adopt the five steps to recovery advocated in this book.

3. Return to work

Patients should not try to return to work unless they score 8 out of 10 for a month. Occasionally, 7 out of 10 is acceptable. **Many patients are made worse by returning to work too early.** The job should not be too physical. Some patients are able to start with 2-3 half-days per week and build up. **This is ideal,** but a lot depends on the type of job and how the patient feels. Most patients are forced to return to half-time work. If a patient has scored 8 out of 10 for a month, this is very likely to be successful. **Patients need to think about returning to work for 1-2 months before they return.** Returning to work requires confidence. If a patient can think about the situations of work and how they may be coped with, confidence is built up. **It is stupid to suddenly decide on Friday night that you will return to work on Monday morning.**

Many patients decide to return to part-time work by deciding on working two full days and one half-day, and resting four full days and one half-day. Although this seems a good idea, **it is likely to fail.** This is because in one full day it is possible to exhaust yourself so much that it takes one week to recover. As stated before, energy is obtained every day, so it is better to return to work as five half-days per week (Figure 22). **To**

RETURN TO WORK

A. 2.5 DAYS

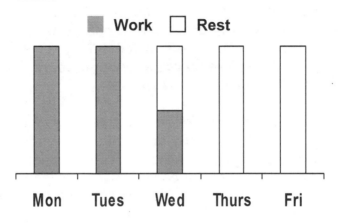

B. 5 HALF DAYS

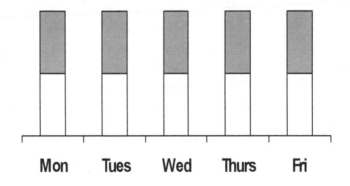

Figure 22   Return to work
It is a mistake to return to part-time work by working 2.5 days,
and resting the rest of the week (A). You can exhaust yourself
in one full day so that you need a week to recover. **It is better**
to work 5 half-days, either mornings or afternoons (B). This is
less likely to totally exhaust you, and you are more likely to
recover from each day's work.

increase your work from half-time to full-time also requires care. In the first two weeks, patients have difficulty in coping with the change. There is a need for relaxation and sleeping, with no social life. The diary may fall to 7, with an occasional 6 out of 10. After 2-3 weeks, the patient feels better and the diary scores return to 8 out of 10. **Before increasing work, scores should remain at 8 out of 10 for 1-2 weeks.**

Ideally, patients should increase working hours only every 6-8 weeks and **providing that diary scores do not get worse.** If scores fall to 5 out of 10, or less, hours should be reduced, as the patient is obviously not coping with work. **When work is increased, the best is every day by one hour.** Thus, patients should work their normal mornings, have their lunch break, and then work an additional hour every day. It is tempting to work a full five-hour stretch each day and miss lunch. This should be resisted as it is a common cause of patients not being able to cope. **The lunch break can be used to have a relaxation session.** Long emotional conversations with people at work are a mistake as they can be very exhausting. Once patients have been ill for some months, they are of great interest to their colleagues. However, recounting **details of your illness or social chat can be more exhausting than working.**

Additional hours are added on in the same way as before, one hour per day over the week. In some cases, a more gradual increase may be indicated. It all depends on the diary scores and maintaining 7-8 out of 10 before increasing your hours. One additional hour on Monday, Wednesday and Friday is a safer alternative to one hour each day of the week. **It is better to do what you feel**

you can do rather than be too ambitious. Better results are obtained more quickly if you make slow progress rather than do too much, have a relapse and go off on sick leave.

4. Change of job
A change of a job is a feature of life today. Retraining and joɓ mobility are not only part of the political climate, they are a result of developments in industry. When a person changes a job, it may be either because his old job has disappeared or that a new job is better. The latter can be associated with great contentment. PVFS patients have to try to see a change of job in a wider context: that many in the community are being forced to do so (albeit not usually for health reasons), and that they should change to a better job **(a job that they can cope with is a better job!).** Nevertheless, a change of job is a major life event and is associated with great stress. It is not a decision that should be undertaken as a result of anger, or a fit of pique. Many patients loved their job before they became ill. These jobs were often difficult and demanding ones which required great energy. **With illness, patients struggle to cope, and one of the first results can be volatile emotions.** Easy irritability can result in sudden outbursts of anger, frustration and tears.

Before a change in job is contemplated, **it is worthwhile to properly assess the situation and its implications.** Ask: was I happy in the job before the illness? If the answer is yes, then consider if the recommendations at the start of this chapter have been given a chance to work. If not, then do so. Also, consider part-time work. For patients unhappy in their work before their illness, **their illness can be a good**

opportunity to change jobs. However, it is still important to consider what is wanted from life, what makes happiness, and what is attainable. **One must be able to cope easily with a new job.** It is unwise at this stage to move to a job that is very demanding.

A change of job is very stressful because of the different environment. Patients need to establish a rapport with their new colleagues to gain goodwill. In previous jobs, patients may have been highly regarded and thus they might have received understanding. Similarly, there is little information on the new environment: Where is the toilet? How does the telephone system work? When is the tea break? Where is the canteen? Where are the envelopes kept? The list of required information can be large. **Patients have to ask for each bit of information and often feel guilty about having to disturb others.** For these reasons, a change of job has to be considered very carefully. It is usually better to persist in the old job until you are better and then change.

PART-TIME EMPLOYMENT

There are greater opportunities for part-time work:

1. Patients in work

For patients happy in their job, **part-time work can be an excellent solution.** It allows them more time to rest. It is positive, as the decision is made in the expectation that health will improve, and that a return to full-time work may be possible. Fortunately, patients with PVFS are often good employees, and employers are usually sympathetic to such a temporary change. Like many other decisions for PVFS patients, **it is best if patients make the decision to do part-time work before they are forced to by the illness.** Sadly, many patients have financial demands which may preclude part-time work. It is often only a reasonable alternative in those families where both partners are at work. After long sick leave, part-time work before full-time employment is best. It allows time for the individual to adjust to the demands of work.

2. Patients not in work

For patients who have been unemployed, a new part-time job is a possibility. However, part-time jobs are very dependant on the country's economic position. They may also be very physically demanding or very stressful; such jobs must be avoided. Taking **any** job is always a weak position from which to start. Try and take jobs that have potential. A PVFS patient cannot "try and see" everything. The nature of the illness is such that a patient needs to use foresight, and **consider all the implications of a decision.**

3. Voluntary work

Where patients are unable to find a suitable part-time/full-time job, they should consider voluntary work. **After a long illness, a patient's confidence is greatly reduced.** The simple routine of an everyday job: getting up early, travelling, speaking to people, being sociable, working, eating and returning home can appear to be an impossible obstacle course. Voluntary work can help to build confidence. The best jobs are those in which hours are flexible; there is little stress on the patient; the work is not physically demanding; and the patient has some control of the working conditions. **These requirements**

are easily fulfilled in most voluntary work. Obviously, a patient may need to choose a suitable job, but there is usually an acceptable selection. If the patient starts with a few hours work per week, it can be quite dramatic how confidence returns. **With greater confidence, there is less anxiety and stress.** A cycle of benefits follow and enjoyment in life starts to return.

UNEMPLOYMENT

This happens. It is not uncommon. For most patients, **unemployment is not sudden, it is probably a product of several months of underperformance.** Many resign through pride, but a few are fired. Such an event, whether the patient jumped or was pushed, is a major life-event. Matters are made worse because PVFS patients were often good workers with an impressive work record. **They feel betrayed.**

It is helpful to consider how this has happened. **For many, it was because they tried to do too much.** They were too ambitious. They exhausted themselves. Exhaustion is a powerful tool for disorientation. A person, disorientated and confused, can behave in an uncharacteristic way. Now, they need time to think and to plan. Unemployment was not a bad card in the game, but rather that the game has ended. For a few, it is just that their illness is so severe that it is incompatible with work. **For most, their own actions have produced a disaster.** In addition, unemployment can be associated with excessive alcohol consumption, depression, suicide or attempted suicide. **All of this ill-health adds to the problems associated with PVFS. It is a deep, deep**

pit. There are two choices: either curl up in a corner, or try and claw a way out. Either option is difficult.

Yet, this can be a great opportunity!! **There is time. Time to rest and recuperate. Time to think and plan.** Not many people are given such an opportunity. Horace (65-8 BC) said: "Adversity has the effect of eliciting talents which in prosperous circumstances would have lain dormant." **The first great benefit, is that the patient rests.** Unfortunately, this may not be beneficial as energy can be lost on emotions. There is self-pity, often manifest by a withdrawing, a crying into the pillow, and a retreat into disturbed sleep. There is shock. Disbelief lasts weeks. During this time the body tries to recover. Unfortunately, much energy is lost with mental activity. **Emotions are up and down; there is mourning for the loss of the job.** These are common reactions for normal individuals, but everything is accentuated and made worse for PVFS patients.

Every patient needs to make the great decision to face life again. For some, this is impossible and they may not work again. For the brave, after 6-8 weeks, they attempt to find some answers. What has happened? Why did it happen? Why did I react like that? What do I want? What will make me happy? What can I get? The vast majority of the population do not have the time to consider such questions. Inscribed on the Temple of Apollo at Delphi, Greece, is a saying ascribed to the Seven Wise Men: **"Know thyself"**. PVFS patients have this fantastic opportunity. Probably less than 5% of the population know themselves, and most who do not are dissatisfied with their job.

Loss of a job is like other great losses in life and is accompanied by a grieving process. **There are predictable stages and effects.** Yet, many feel that their experience is unique and others could not possibly understand their situation. Although this may be comforting for the patient, it is untrue. As I have had to deal with many patients with great losses (unemployment, end of relationships, failure at exams, financial ruin, betrayal, etc) I wrote the book: "**Climbing Out of the Pit of Life"**, Dodona Books, 1995 (ISBN 0-9511090-49). In this book, the ladder (**l**ifeless, **a**nger, **d**enial, **d**isgrace, **e**ndeavour, **r**enewal) **describes the stages of deep loss and how to progress from each stage to the next.** It is possible to climb out of the pit, and use the opportunity to gain strength and happiness. PVFS patients should be **honest** about their situation. **They should decide how they want to live, and if they are prepared to climb the difficult ladder to recovery.** The plan advocated in this book is not easy. However, many patients have been greatly helped. I am always amazed at how much can be achieved by a willingness to learn, especially from past mistakes.

SOCIAL SECURITY BENEFITS

Accepting social security benefits is still something which many patients find difficult. There is the "stigma" attached to not working, perhaps made worse by the individual's own attitudes before the illness. Again, the lack of visible evidence of disability can make others think that the patient is work-shy or malingering. This is yet another time when patients need to realise that they are ill, accept the consequences, and ignore those who do not understand. **Those accepting benefits and help**

146

often feel persecuted. Stories in newspapers revealing "scroungers" do not help; instead, they contribute to a general feeling that "handouts" must only go to those in need. The logic is that if there is a system with frequent checks, only those in real need will stand up to these investigations. **The logic is flawed.** Many of the needy, and some with PVFS, do not have the physical and mental resources to stand up to these checks.

A patient may be more exhausted by getting a benefit than not getting it. For example, a patient receiving invalidity benefit will periodically be summoned to attend a medical assessment. Occasionally, at such a medical, the medical officer may decide that the patient is capable of work. This decision can be a great shock to patients, and even convince them that society is against them. **This is not so, it is the system that is at fault.** Many patients have struggled up many flights of stairs to attend a medical examination. To the patients this was essential as they needed to attend, and often they were reknown for their reliability before illness. Sadly, their arrival at the examination was their downfall. The medical officer would simply say: "If you got up the flights of stairs to attend, you cannot be ill". The fact that the patient may be in bed for weeks after this event is of little consequence to the system. **When dealing with the system, patients should not do what they cannot normally do.** If patients had not climbed the stairs, they probably would have got their benefits.

The system, because of society's attitudes, works on **frequent checks, double-checks, appeals and adjudications.** A recommendation of being incapable of work is only the first step. Immediately, the patient's

147

general practitioner can issue a new sick note, and the whole procedure of reassessment will be started. A patient's doctor is his greatest ally. The system is generally fair and can work well, but there are also failures. The best explanations of the system are in **Dr Charles Shepherd's** book, "Living with ME", Vermilion, 1999 and **Dr Anne Macintyre's** book, "Chronic Fatigue Syndrome: how to live with it", Thorsons, 1998. Self-help groups are invaluable in this maze of rules and regulations:

a)   **M.E. Association,** 4 Top Angel, Buckingham, MK18 1TH. Tel: 0870 444 8233

b)   **Action for M.E.** Canningford House, 38 Victoria Street, Bristol, BS1 6BY. Tel: 0845 123 2314

CONCLUSION

Time off, or part-time work may be necessary, however, this should not be regarded as a solution to the patient's problems. **Instead, it is an opportunity to test how much can be done.** Often, with time off, a patient can become so worried and preoccupied with not improving that he does not attempt to see what he can do. Initially, it is best to look upon part-time work as "test periods" rather than "solutions". **PVFS patients should use their brains more than their muscles;** it recovers first and it uses less energy. Because of the need to avoid wasted effort, patients have to identify their priorities. **The combination of thinking first, and concentrating on the important areas of life is a winning formula.**

SUMMARY

1.	Employment is important and valuable. To keep a job: stop unnecessary exertion; minimise all walking; think before any action; adopt unwind techniques and increase sleep; and stop all social engagements.

2.	If patients require sick leave, they should plan on at least 3 months, often it is 6-9 months. For recovery, do not substitute other activities for work.

3.	Returning to work requires careful planning. Ideally, part-time work is recommended with a slow increase in the hours of work, being guided by the patient's diary.

4.	A change of job can be a good or bad decision. Consider carefully the implications. Take a job in which it is easy to cope.

5.	Part-time work is useful for many patients when they are having difficulties with their job. It is also the recommended route for a return to work.

6.	Voluntary work is frequently the ideal way of returning to the work routine with a minimum of stress and anxiety. Confidence can quickly return.

7.	Social security benefits are complicated. Know the system and what is being expected of you. Get advice early and do not be naïve.

Important facts

To be successful in keeping your job you need a good strategy. Good use of sick leave, unemployment and part-time work require knowledge of the illness and its effects on the body. Patients need to take matters seriously and have specific plans. Previous attitudes to work must change.

CHAPTER THIRTEEN
YOUNG PEOPLE

When I first started seeing PVFS patients, they were all middle-aged adults. It was believed that the illness did not occur in young people. However, after the illness **became more understood, illness in the young was recognised and validated**. This was some 5 years later, and shows that medical practice changes slowly. I have no doubt that illness in young people has always been present. The problem was that it was not recognised. All ages can be affected (Figure 1), but the illness is less common in young people compared to adults. There is also the perception that children are happier than adults. I believe that this is true, **because young people take every opportunity to be happy.** Unfortunately, there is a down-side. Sometimes adults feel that young people should be always happy – even when they are ill. This is wrong.

It is important to recognise the special needs of young people. This has been superbly done by **Jane Colby**, a former headmistress. Her book provides essential information for parents, schools and health professionals[15]. She is also the Executive Director of the national charity **TYMES** (The Young ME Sufferer). This independent organisation for young people has been a great success. Young people are given a forum for interaction and discussion. In addition, the newsletter and website offer support, informative articles and advice.

In many ways I find that young people are easier to manage than adults. **This is because the relationship is not as complicated, and the young are easier to convince of a sensible course of action.** My approach with young people is as for adults with an emphasis on staying within your energy limits and the daily diary. However, there are some important differences. As parents are involved, it is important that the same message is given to the child from both parents and myself. Often, it is more difficult to convince the parents of the best course of action. Best results are achieved when everybody is working together. I try and see parents and the child at the start of the consultation, then the child alone and then everyone at the end. **It is important to always see the child alone and hear what he/she has to say.**

LEARNING

Both parents and child have to embark on a course of learning. **They have to learn about the illness and from each other.** Success depends on:

1. Honesty
Young people are great realists. They see things as

152

they are, and are not as conditioned as adults. They face reality and do not pretend. Therefore, **adults should not try and protect young people, but be honest and truthful.** Then, a good strategy can be worked out and better recovery from the illness guaranteed. If one is honest, even with children as young as 5 years, a helpful relationship can develop. This should not be surprising as young children throughout time have been able to deal with disasters. This approach must be emphasised as recovery depends on the cooperation of the child. **The parent cannot do what is required for the child.** The parent is able to only help. Many recoveries have been delayed by parents being protective of their children.

Honesty by all parties is also the fundamental basis for learning. PVFS is not incurable. **Resolution depends on sticking to the management plan,** and this cannot be achieved through lies. Diary scores must reflect reality, and both parent and child must start to learn from the diary scores how much energy is being used on what activities. Honest discussion of these matters can greatly aid the speed of recovery, and can be fun.

2. Clear limits

In growing up, children have the job of testing the limits to which they can push their parents. Parents have the responsibility of setting clear limits to what is acceptable behaviour. Although it can be very annoying when children test a parent's resolve in keeping these limits, it is necessary. Thus if bedtime is 9.30pm, the child will try to extend this time and the parent should ensure it is kept unless there are extenuating circumstances. **I come across many parents who set limits but then allow the child to break them.** For PVFS, this is a disaster.

153

Children in this situation will have great difficulty in recovering. A way of setting these clear limits could be in the form of contracts. **I like contracts and deals.** I have always made them with my children and I make them with patients. It works very well. It works because it is really the "barter" system which was in existence before money. When there are two people, one does something for the other, and the latter returns the favour by doing something else. **The simple system of contracts is loved by children and prepares them for life in the real world.**

How young people spend their time is just as important as in adults. Over the last years, the single greatest change in management has been **the need to regulate young people's use of television, videos, computer games and music.** Parents have the job of ensuring limits on these activities are kept. This approach cannot be emphasised too much. In the past, as these activities did not involve physical exertion, they were deemed to be "rest". This is wrong as there is great mental use of energy. I have seen too many people who spend all day in bed "resting" while watching television, videos, listening to music and playing computer games. **These young people do not recover.** These activities have to be regulated into half hour periods, and preceded by boredom periods. **There should be no more than one and a half hours of music _or_ a video in any one day.** If scores are under 5/10, there should be no computer games. **These rules have to be explained to young people, and parents must insist on their implementation.** It is like all good parenting and not unlike the rule that a young person must be home by 10 o'clock at night. **Visitors are also a great use of**

energy. I have known young people in bed all day with a continuous stream of their friends visiting them. These patients do not recover. Bed is for lying down with your eyes closed and with no noise in the room. Nothing else will do. Visitors should be regulated to no more than two per day **and** only if there is a better score than the previous average. **Visitors should not stay more than 45 minutes.** This is not a holiday camp, it is about an ill person wanting to get better.

3. Assessment

Assessment of progress must be honest: one does not tell children that they are getting better when they are not. Such assessments must be objective, and this is why I believe in the daily diary. This daily assessment is a great test of progress and recovery. **Many parents want to do the diary for the child.** This is wrong. Children as young as 5 years can be taught to do a diary. Sometimes it means that symbols have to be used. However, as with adults, **the patient is the one who is required to do the daily diary.** This emphasises the importance of the diary, and also brings home to children how they may use the diary for recovery. All of the chapters on the five steps to better recovery apply to young people. **They need to understand energy.** Energy is gained in the same way as adults. There is the need for at least 10 hours sleep. There is the need for trying to teach the patient the art of unwinding. Indeed in many cases, young people have found it easier to learn the art of unwinding compared to adults.

Energy is more easily lost as a child. Fortunately, this is physical energy, and **children lose mental energy much less than adults.** Children do not have the anger and frustration of adults. They also do not ruminate and dwell on subjects, the way older PVFS patients do. Again, they are not as stressed as adults. Unfortunately, **the emotional energy of relationships can be worse in children.** There can be great attempts to get their own way, with much crying and tantrums. At these times, it is important for parents to be firm and not give in to the child's demands. If this occurs, greater problems are created for the future. No matter how tired the parent has become, there cannot be a surrender to the child. This consistent behaviour is the greatest help a parent can give.

Energy must be made to last. As in adults, **boredom periods are very important.** Over the years, I found that children accept boredom periods more easily than adults. Then, it occurred to me that boredom periods are an integral part of a child's life. How many times are children made to sit or be quiet when it is the opposite of what they want to do? Simply, **children are already conditioned to boredom periods.** So, yet again, for children the steps to better recovery are already a part of their life. **The required change in lifestyle is much less than in an adult.** This is reflected in that children recover in greater numbers and faster than adults.

4. Prizes and rewards

In life good progress and hard work can result in prizes and rewards. When there is a reward as a result of no effort, it is not appreciated. **I believe in rewards for learning and effort;** and if this does not happen there should be no prizes. I have frequently come across the parent who is trying to cheer the child up by buying new presents. Usually, the child is unwell because he has not stayed within his energy levels. The child is then faced with further mental stimulation by the new present. The child is not very enthusiastic about the present as he is too tired. The parent feels hurt and resolves to spend even more money on the next present. **The vicious cycle is repeated, and made worse.**

My approach is to ask children to stay within their energy limits. This will be reflected in the daily diary scores. If they manage to do well over a week, they deserve a reward. **The child should specify the reward and it should not be too expensive,** a special magazine is ideal. If the child's diary scores are not better, the child does not get a reward. **One should not give the reward irrespective of progress.** This is not a game in which what you do does not matter. It is not about just taking part, it is about winning. Rewards are given only to winners.

If a child has had a really bad week, for example with an infection, it is reasonable for there to be a small present. One would do the same with an adult, perhaps with a present such as a small bar of chocolate. However, **I must say that I believe a long cuddle or telling them a funny joke is much more helpful.** Christmas and birthday presents always create difficulties. **Parents often believe that the ill child should get the most expensive present.** This can result in jealousy if there are other children in the family. I believe that the ill child should be subject to the same rules as the rest of the family. After all, in later life, equal treatment of all is supposed to be an objective of society. Therefore I do not believe in buying the child a toy shop (Figure 23). Instead, I believe in carefully chosen

Figure 23 Many or one?
Parents are tempted to give their children a toy shop. One special toy is better, uses less concentration, is more appreciated and is cheaper. The parent needs to spend time thinking of what the child needs.

presents rather than expensive ones. **The key is to give children presents that they need.**

Parental income is not an important factor in a child's recovery. The most important factor is the time that a parent spends with a child. If parents give freely of their time, there will always be great benefits to children. More importantly, this applies if the children are ill, poor, or healthy.

SCHOOL

Most parents have a great worry of young people missing school. This is reasonable but does not help matters. My position is that **all that is learnt up to 11 years at school can be learnt in one good year.** From 11-18 years, the work can be learnt in two good years. Therefore **my objective is to get the young person well rather than worry about lost time at school.** I have seen many parents trying to encourage young people to return to school when they are only 5/10 in their diary scores. Others have insisted that the school provide home tutors. My approach is for the young person to understand energy and return to school when the diary scores are 8/10. **If this is done there is sustained recovery.** Each time a young person tries to return to school and fails, confidence is destroyed in the person, the parents, school and doctor. If the plan in this book is followed, a return to school should be possible in 10-12 months. Then, all work can be learnt and no time will be lost. **As always, does one focus on a single objective (getting better) or have many** (getting better, going to school, doing well, etc)?

The difficulties at school are not only with learning. If this were so, a return to school would not be too difficult. However, school also involves considerable physical activities (walking to classes, stairs, etc) and mental activities (explaining the illness to friends, saying no to sport, parties, etc). In addition, there are all the other problems of the young, such as peer group pressure, teasing, rivalry, jealousy etc. As with working, if a patient is at school and scoring 5/10, it is easier to remain at school. **Choice of subjects is very important:** mathematics needs a lot of concentration; some subjects (eg geography, history) require a good memory; english and social sciences can be recommended. In some schools, it is possible for the student to do only mornings. **All that is said on the chapter on employment applies to school.** It must be remembered that all of a young person's life needs to be considered and not only school.

COLLEGE/UNIVERSITY

To go to university is an ambition of many people. Their parents are proud of them and there is great hope and adventure in their lives. To drop out of university because of illness is a great disaster. As with school, there is initial optimism that the long summer holidays will result in recovery. **When this does not happen, there is anxiety and depression.** The first thing to recognise is if one had to drop out of university, recovery will take many months. The usual course is that an individual needs a year to deal with the illness. The plan as described in this book requires total commitment. There is no time for a social life or attempts to keep up with university work. **A total change of lifestyle is required.**

The aim is to get the diary scores back to 8/10. It will take time and an understanding of energy. As many university students are smart, they frequently think that there is an easy way. I do not know of an easy way. **The steps in this book are not easy.**

A return to university, as a return to work, must not be underestimated. The course content has to be examined: is it possible to do fewer subjects, especially initially? can the mix of subjects be changed? All aspects of accommodation must be considered: is it possible to get into halls of residence? can the bedroom be close to the dining hall? who will be making the meals? **Time must be taken to consider the practical aspects of a return to university life.** If this is not done, the previous mistakes can be easily repeated. Extracurricular activities must be stopped for the first term back. **The object is not to let scores fall below 7/10.**

During the vacation, there should be no holiday jobs unless scores have averaged 8/10. This can be very hard for students, but with no social life, financial spending is greatly reduced. **Financial gains are not better than good health.** Nevertheless, young people at university recover faster and more predictably than other adults. Their bodies are younger, more resilient and heal faster. **This is especially so if it is possible to focus their intellect on getting better.**

THE FUTURE

It is helpful here to consider how one progresses from a child to an adult (Figure 24). As an adult, it is hoped that one has become mature by accepting personal

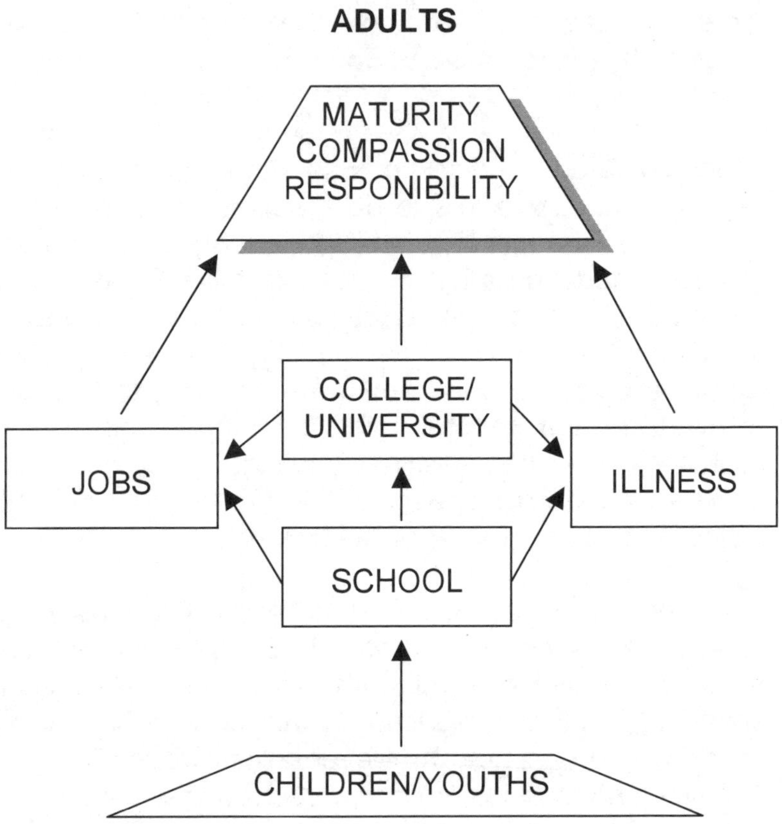

ADULTS

MATURITY
COMPASSION
RESPONIBILITY

COLLEGE/
UNIVERSITY

JOBS

ILLNESS

SCHOOL

CHILDREN/YOUTHS

Figure 24   Adult skills
Life involves progress from a child to an adult.   There are
many ways of learning the skills required for adulthood
(responsibility, compassion and maturity).   School,
College/University work for some.   But, employment and
illness can also achieve the same results.

responsibility and acquiring compassion for others. There are many ways in which this can be achieved. Indeed, one can say that **illness may be a fast track to adulthood.** It is certainly a great teacher to those who want to prepare for adulthood. What is missing in Figure 24 is the statement that one only becomes educated and trained at college or university. In the past, university students were guaranteed jobs, but this is no longer true. I meet very many young people who have completed university but still do not know what job they want. I believe that **students should know what job they want before they go to university.** Several PVFS patients have found that once they drop out of university, they recognise that they should not have been there in the first place. This is another example of how illness may ultimately save time and expense.

Almost all PVFS patients who have recovered and returned to school or university were able to quickly catch up. I believe that this was because **illness had focused their thoughts and they were now more committed.** They knew what they wanted out of life and what they did not. Often in life, we need good reasons to work harder and better. Many in the population go through school and university without asking if this is what they want to do. **With illness, the effort to stay at university is great and is usually unsuccessful unless it is what the patient wants.**

SUMMARY

1.   Both parents and child have to learn about PVFS and how to plan recovery. Adults should not try and protect young people but be truthful and

honest. The parent cannot do what is required of the child.

2.   Parents have to set clear limits and need to regulate the use of television, videos, computer games and music. Visitors use up much energy and must be restricted.

3.   Progress needs to be regularly assessed by the daily diary. Young people have to do the diary themselves, even if it means using symbols.

4.   The system of contracts, prizes/rewards is easily understood by young people. There should be no reward for lack of progress.

5.   Children quickly catch up time lost at school so all efforts should be focused on getting children better.

6.   Students who drop out of university because of illness need to change their lifestyle.

7.   Illness allows young people to become mature by accepting personal responsibility and acquiring compassion for others.

Important facts

Recovery in young people depends on them taking responsibilities (especially for the diary). Parents must set clear limits and ensure these are kept. There must not be rewards for lack of progress. College/university students should use their intellect to get better. With illness young people can become mature and compassionate.

CHAPTER FOURTEEN
ALTERNATIVE MEDICINE

With PVFS, most doctors cannot agree on any one treatment. Thus, there are very many management approaches. Some treatments work for some people, but do not work for others. **Many treatments do not work at all.** Each week I am aware of a new treatment. Nearly all of these treatments are not tested and cannot be recommended. Alternative medicine often has success rates of 0-30%; whereas in modern medicine with agents such as antibiotics, the success rate can be more than 90%. **A lower success rate can mean that a patient may never find success.**

Whenever there have been groups of people, there has always been a need to have an alternative. In previous editions, I have discussed alternative therapies in some detail. However, in this edition, I shall focus on the principles of treatments as there are many other books that can provide the reader with greater details. This is an area of "fringe" medicine. **There are few objective comparisons of the treatment with established medical practice.**

CONSIDERATIONS

It is important for patients to be aware of:

1. Cost

Many treatments are outside the National Health Service and so patients have to pay. **It is believed that patients who pay are more appreciative.** Unfortunately, some treatments can be very expensive. There are tragic stories of PVFS patients who have been made bankrupt. **Patients should not have unrealistic expectations of treatment.** It is totally understandable that patients want to get better, but paying for treatment does not guarantee recovery.

2. Advantages

Alternative practitioners usually have several advantages over medical practitioners. They spend a lot of time with the patient, listen carefully to the complaints and are very sympathetic. The prescribed treatment appears individual for the patient. The patient has a much more positive experience from the consultation. In addition, **it is not unusual to have several alternative treatments prescribed if one does not work.**

3. Philosophy

One criticism of modern medicine is that doctors can be too specialised and tend to focus on one complaint or a specific part of the body. In contrast, **alternative medicine can be seen to be holistic, considering the whole body's health.** In this chapter, I shall consider treatments that are historic, those that deal with the mind, and then those that deal with foods and toxins.

HISTORIC TREATMENTS

There is the misconception that alternative medicine is new. In fact, an alternative practice such as acupuncture has been in existence for 2000 years. **Thus, much of traditional medicine is comparatively new.** Perhaps because of their long history, alternative medicine practices are better at explaining illness to the lay public: "imbalance of energy", "presence of toxins", "natural remedies" etc. **The public appreciates the time which alternative practitioners take to explain their treatment.** This can be quite refreshing compared to the more paternalistic attitudes of traditional medicine.

1. Homeopathy
This is derived from two Greek words, "homois" and "pathos", meaning "similar" and "suffering". A homeopathic remedy is one that is able to produce symptoms in a healthy person which are similar to those in an ill patient. **The treatment is aimed at stimulating the bodily defences in patients to bring about a recovery.** Much of the initial concepts and knowledge of homeopathy were recorded by Samuel Hahnemann (1755-1843). Homeopathic treatment is available within the National Health Service and there is a Faculty of Homeopathy, recognised by an Act of Parliament. A brief history is available[16].

I believe that **homeopathy has an important role** in the management of some problems. Homeopathy was effective when there were many infectious diseases, and when there was no specific treatment. The situation is similar to that with PVFS. Some PVFS patients have had considerable relief of symptoms with homeopathic remedies. **Any approach to treatment that has lasted nearly 200 years cannot be lightly dismissed.**

2. Acupuncture
Acupuncture has been in existence for over 2,000 years. Chinese medicine sees all the world as a balance between two opposing forces (Yin and Yang). Taoism ("the way") is the means by which there is harmony between man and these forces. **Illness is a result of disharmony.** Thus, patients often saw their doctor when they were well, and paid the doctor to keep them in harmony. **The success of acupuncture in a patient depends on the skill of the acupuncturist and the complaint.** Best results are in those who have a benefit after the first treatment. **Acupuncture is most effective in pain relief.** The way acupuncture acts is unknown; it may release natural mediators (e.g. endorphins which are natural opiates).

3. Spiritual (Psychic) Healing
The healing of one person by another, by a technique unknown to modern medicine, is usually part of a ritual such as "laying-on of hands". **Some healers activate the patient's own energy, whilst other healers transmit their own (or their God's) energy to the patient.** There are numerous, well-documented reports in religious and medical texts. It is not often successful. When it works, it cannot be explained (i.e. a miracle). Some of my patients have followed the recovery path as in Figure 25. **Despite doing all the right things, patients appear to have poor recovery.** Then, something happens and this is especially the case with spiritual healing, and the patient suddenly recovers to what was expected. There are two important

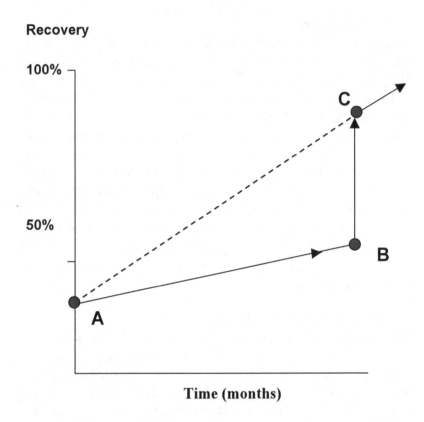

Figure 25 Recovery with time
Sometimes I have seen patients do all the right things but only
have poor recovery (AB). I would have expected better
recovery (AC). At B, something happens (such as laying-on of
hands) and there is recovery to what would have been
expected (AC).

observations: recovery is never better than would be expected; and future progress is along the predicted line of recovery. It seems that a **patient's belief may somehow unlock their progress.**

4. Massage

Touching is a necessary activity for a normal healthy life. **Massage is the ancient art of healing by touch.** Very many ancient Chinese, Indian and Egyptian practitioners have described their art in great detail. Massage is a complicated subject and patients who are interested should get more information from books on the subject. **Acupressure** and **Shiatsu** (finger pressure) are like acupuncture without needles. One presses with the thumb over specific points for 20 seconds, releases and waits for 10 seconds, and then repeats up to 5 times. Pressure on the inside of the left wrist is useful for nausea. Pressure on the middle of the upper lip helps pain. Pressure on the lobe of the left ear helps sleep. Some patients have found these techniques to be very helpful. **Aromatherapy** uses essential oils (aromatic chemicals) and is often combined with massage. The **Alexander technique** focuses on postural improvement to cure or prevent many disorders. **Reflexology** is an ancient Chinese and Egyptian technique which unblocks energy channels throughout the body.

T'ai Chi has become very popular. It is based on the balance between the opposing forces of **Yin** (dark, feminine, passive) and **Yang** (light, male, active). Yin represents the interior of the body and solid organs, whereas Yang represents the exterior of the body and hollow organs. **T'ai** is the Chinese word meaning a centre point which is the dividing line between Yin and

Yang. **Chi** is the energy force of life. The Taoists believe that if you can release and direct the energy force within the body, by a series of exercises, the balance in the body is regained and so stress and illness can be removed.

MIND TECHNIQUES

Mind techniques have a long history and have become more popular recently. Patients gain energy through sleep and unwind techniques (Chapter Nine). **All patients benefit from adopting an unwind technique.** My particular favourite (EMBME) is described in my book ("Unwind" 1991, Dodona Books). **In addition, in "Unwind", Eastern techniques (meditation, Buddhism, Taoism, Zen and Yoga) are described.** The place of Western techniques (Christianity, Psychotherapy, Auto-suggestion, Hypnotherapy, Biofeedback and Visualisation) are also explained. Unwind techniques are very highly recommended. The difficulty for most patients is that unwind techniques take time to learn; benefits are not felt for 2-3 months. **During this period, patients need to commit themselves to learning a new skill.** Sadly, many patients who have been ill for years are not prepared to learn; they expect to be cured instantly.

1. Meditation
Meditation is a component of many Eastern techniques and can include a wide range of activities. One definition is: **"a family of techniques which have in common a conscious attempt to focus attention in a non-analytical way and an attempt not to dwell on ruminating discursive thought".** Unwind techniques,

aided by controlled breathing and quiet chanting, are common to most forms of meditation. **The object is to get out of the "fight or flight" (i.e. stress) reaction of modern living.** Apart from the mental peace of such a procedure, there appears to be reduced sympathetic nervous response. Blood pressure, muscle tone and skin conductance also may be lowered. Thus, the whole process is high quality rest; the muscles and the mind are given the right environment for repair of damaged tissues. It is not surprising that all patients can benefit from meditation.

2. Self-hypnosis
In hypnosis, a trance-like state is induced in which the mind accepts suggestions. There is total mental concentration but physical relaxation. **Hypnotism is not a treatment in itself.** It is important to recognise that hypnosis is the acceptance of suggestion. It can be very useful in dealing with stress and increasing an individual's ability to unwind or deal with the illness.

FOODS

Food is an important factor in recovery from PVFS. There is no doubt that some patients on bizarre diets (ice-cream and chips, cauliflower and sugar etc) may develop nutritional deficiencies. For patients who have a normal diet and are eating within a family, such nutritional deficiencies are rare. **However, there are useful foods:**

1. Herbalism
The use of plants in healing probably dates from man's earliest existence. There are many "decoctions" (prepared by boiling) which can be used for many of the

complaints of PVFS patients. Certainly, many modern medicines have been derived from plants, however in PVFS it has been difficult to assess herbal remedies.

2. Royal Jelly
Royal Jelly is the food for the Queen Bee. **It is special and for centuries it has been used to treat a variety of ailments.** Sadly, there are two major drawbacks. The effects are not predictable; and ordinary honey can be sold as Royal Jelly. However, many benefit from the fact that Royal Jelly can relax them and help sleep. Others claim a reduction in muscle pain and the ability to think more clearly.

3. Probiotics
Probiotics are bacteria which are "friendly" and can replace more harmful bacteria in the colon. These bacteria are concentrated in capsules or in drinks to be taken in between meals. **The bacteria then multiply in the colon and displace other more harmful agents.** Some of these bacteria eg **Lactobacillus acidophilus**, are also found in live yoghurt. They are killed in pasteurised yoghurt and so are of no use. Yoghurt is a very easily digested food and can be recommended for PVFS patients.

TOXINS

1. Dental Amalgam Removal
Mercury is present in **dental amalgam** which is used for filling teeth. In individuals with very many fillings, **it has been suggested that removal of these fillings can get rid of PVFS symptoms.** Unfortunately, removal of all fillings cannot be done on the National Health Service

and may cost several thousand pounds. In addition, removal of the amalgam causes a large amount of mercury to be released; and such dental procedures may result in a patient having a relapse. It is very unlikely that many patients will benefit from amalgam removal, and I would not recommend it.

2. Colonic Lavage

During the early 1990's, colonic lavage was very popular. **The reasoning is that the large colon can become overloaded with toxins and the patient requires repeated enemas to remove these toxins.** An alternative name for this treatment is colonic irrigation. A colonic therapist will insert a large volume of warm water through the anus into the large bowel, removal of the water is accompanied by faeces and toxins. This treatment can be very expensive. It cannot be recommended.

CONCLUSION

One criticism of modern medicine is that it is too specialised. Doctors become experts on a particular part of the body or particular illnesses. **They appear to know more and more about less and less.** Some feel that this approach has resulted in doctors being narrow-minded, and even short-sighted. **The techniques mentioned in this chapter are different. They consider the whole person, not just a symptom or a part of the body.** They are also of another time; most have existed for hundreds of years. In the past, specific drug therapy was not available, and there were also many infectious diseases. Successful treatment depended on understanding the whole person and using all of the body's resources to fight the illness.

What should a patient do? The answer depends on the patient. Throughout this book, I have suggested that patients should become responsible for their own health. In time, they will know more about their illness in relation to their bodies than their doctor. Similarly, as alternative medical techniques have not been fully tested (or accepted) by the medical profession, patients may easily acquire more information than their doctor. **If a patient feels that he should try alternative medicine, then he should.** But, before he does, he should make one commitment – he should promise to be honest. If after a reasonable time (say 3-4 weeks); there is no improvement, then, he should be honest enough to admit that the treatment has not worked. **To try is to live, but one must always be honest in assessing the results.**

SUMMARY

1.   There has always been a need for alternatives and patients appreciate the time alternative practitioners take to explain their treatments.

2.   Alternative medicine is often "older" than traditional medicine, but the success rates are 0-30% as compared to more than 90% in traditional medicine.

3.   Patients should not have unrealistic expectations and should not pay more than they can afford.

4. Historic treatments (homeopathy, acupuncture, spiritual healing, massage and T'ai Chi) usually have good results.

5. Mind techniques (meditation and self-hypnosis) also usually have good results. Food and removal of toxins are fashionable but usually have poor results.

6. Patients need to choose if they should try a particular technique. There are more techniques than patients, but I feel understanding energy is the most difficult but the most successful.

Important facts

There are hundreds of alternative remedies. Their success rate varies between 0% and 30%, and they can be very expensive. An understanding of energy is the best route to recovery.

CHAPTER FIFTEEN

LYME BORRELIOSIS AND PVFS

Lyme Borreliosis is named after the town in the United States where an outbreak of juvenile arthritis occurred in 1975. In 1982, the causative organism (*Borrelia burgdorferi*) was identified and found to be a spirochaete. It is very likely that this organism has been around for thousands of years. **So, why has it not been recognised before?** The answer is probably in that it is transmitted to humans from ticks[17], and humans are now more exposed to ticks by their activities. Camping, hill walking, bird watching, etc, are all invasions into tick territory that can result in infection unless appropriate precautions are taken[17]. **If you have not had a tick bite, you cannot get Lyme Borreliosis.**

There is a lot of information on the Internet about Lyme Borreliosis. Some of this information is good, some incorrect and some dangerous. **It is very difficult for patients to identify accurate information.** Matters are made worse as there is disagreement on what is correct among medical practitioners. This chapter gives the view of the majority of the medical profession and that of our laboratory which provides a national testing service for Lyme Borreliosis. **Fortunately, among the medical profession there is more agreement than disagreement (Figure 26).**

Terminology is also confusing. Historically **Lyme Disease** was used but patients may be asymptomatic and so this is not appropriate. **Lyme Borreliosis (LB)** refers to those individuals who have *Borrelia burgdorferi* infection. There is also *Lyme neuroborreliosis* where there is neurological involvement. For ease of reference, I shall use LB to describe the infection and illness.

CLINICAL FEATURES

The clinical features of LB can be similar to those of PVFS. This has produced confusion with **many PVFS patients thinking that they have LB.** It must first be emphasised that infection is transmitted from tick bites. Some of the early stages of the tick can be difficult to recognise as they are very small (diameter of a pinhead) and are colourless until their blood meal. Thus, some patients do not recall a tick bite, however, **all patients must have been in tick country.** Those individuals living in city centres and who do not go into the country will not have LB. In Britain, many areas have no ticks infected. Where there is infection, 1-30% of the ticks are infected. Thus, with most tick bites, there is only a small chance of infection.

After an infected tick bite, infection follows 3-32 days later. **Early LB** is characterised by the typical rash

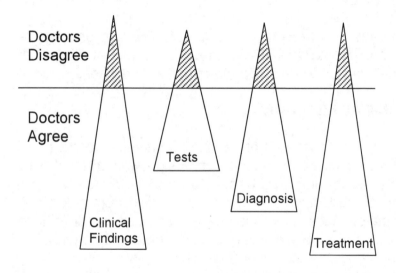

Figure 26   Lyme borreliosis and doctors
The majority of doctors agree on the clinical findings, tests, diagnosis and treatment of Lyme Borreliosis.   A minority disagree.

(called erythema migrans). It starts as a raised red swelling around the tick bite which gradually expands with central clearing to produce a **"target lesion"**. Other skin and neurological complaints described in PVFS can occur. Many patients do not have a rash. Fever, malaise, fatigue and lymph node enlargement are common.

Late LB is becoming more recognised. Usually, complaints are of skin, musculoskeletal and neurological involvement. These complaints can show great similarity to PVFS, especially with extreme fatigue, poor concentration and memory. Chronic joint swelling and pain can become disabling and resistant to treatment. Nevertheless, most patients gradually get better and those resistant to treatment are a small minority. In most cases, **LB patients have a better prognosis than in those patients without an identifiable cause of their PVFS symptoms.**

INVESTIGATIONS

Laboratory tests are necessary investigations in late LB. Unfortunately, both the laboratory and the test require careful consideration.

1. Laboratories
In Britain, within the National Health Service, there are only a few laboratories offering LB tests. Specialist confirmatory tests are usually only done in the accredited laboratories in Southampton and Inverness. There are several other unaccredited laboratories which offer LB testing. In North America, Europe and Britain there are accreditation systems in place for laboratories. **These**

systems **ensure that each laboratory test is reproducible, accurate** and that there are appropriate internal and external quality assurance schemes. Therefore in such laboratories, the user can be confident of the test result. Many private laboratories are not accredited and therefore **the user cannot be confident of the result.** This is a particular problem in LB diagnosis.

2. Tests

For LB, a two step procedure is usually recommended. This means that an initial test, usually an enzyme-linked immunosorbent assay (ELISA) is used for screening. This result is then confirmed by Western Blotting. The screening test is sensitive and therefore there are many false positives. Thus, up to 30% of ELISA positive samples may not be confirmed by Western Blotting. All tests may be limited by the antigen being used in the test. Therefore, it is **important that local antigens are used, and tests are validated on the local population.** In a few clinical situations, a Polymerase Chain Reaction test is performed.

It is important to emphasise that the adoption of the two step procedure in diagnosis was a major advance. This increased the confidence in the diagnosis for most individuals; and this increased effectiveness of diagnosis will not be as dramatic in the future. **Failures in diagnosis do not apply to all situations equally.** In early LB, diagnosis is limited because antibodies may take 6-8 weeks to develop or early antibiotic treatment may have prevented the development of antibody. As these limitations do not apply to late LB, **almost all late LB cases will have positive serological tests.**

Unfortunately, many individuals who are not diagnosed with LB but feel that they have infection, use the information that applies to early LB to justify their late LB situation. When one considers **LB as the cause of PVFS, it is late LB** and therefore the serological tests are positive in almost all cases. Some laboratories offer direct microscopy and various immunofluorescent tests. These tests are only dependable if they are offered in an accredited laboratory. Often, patients have to pay for these tests and like many private allergy tests, the results are not dependable.

DIAGNOSIS

This can be very difficult and is the reason why many patients are not definitively diagnosed with LB.

1. Clinical picture.
The clinical picture of LB can be similar to many other medical conditions. The vast array of signs and symptoms also complicate any medical assessment. Nevertheless, the characteristic rash of erythema migrans is diagnostic, but many patients do not have this characteristic rash. In America and Europe the rash may be more common than in Britain. Of all the clinical signs and symptoms, **the characteristic rash is the only diagnostic sign of LB.** Other clinical presentations are not diagnostic.

2. Medical Assessment.
In the vast majority of cases, diagnosis is made by a medical assessment of the clinical picture and laboratory investigations. This depends on the experience of the doctor and as more doctors become aware of the

presence of LB, the diagnosis is made more often. As with all medical conditions, **the doctor has the responsibility of excluding other causes of the patients' complaints.** In early LB, the emphasis is on the clinical presentation as laboratory tests may be negative. However, in late LB, the **laboratory tests are very likely to be positive.** The diagnosis is therefore made on a combination of clinical presentation, exclusion of other causes of the illness, and a positive laboratory test.

3. Trial of treatment.
In some cases when it is difficult to make the diagnosis of LB, there is a short three week trial of oral antibiotics. If this produces a significant improvement, a presumptive diagnosis of LB can be made. In a very small number of patients, the trial may be of three weeks with parenteral (intramuscular or intravenous) antibiotics. Again, **the improvement must be significant (greater than 30%).** In patients with LB, the improvement can be greater than 70%. Small improvements are probably due to the placebo effect.

MANAGEMENT

As there is no definitive test for LB, there is not complete agreement among medical practitioners on the best management. This is complicated by many patients not having LB but feeling that they have this condition. Nevertheless, there is far more agreement among doctors than disagreement (Figure 26).

1. Short courses of antibiotics.
Everyone agrees that for early LB, a 2-3 week course of

oral antibiotics is the treatment of choice. Doxycycline is the antibiotic of choice, but amoxicillin or erythromycin can be used. In severe cases parenteral antibiotics (ceftriaxone or penicillin) are indicated[17,18]. When patients have LB, **there is a dramatic improvement in symptoms** and there is complete recovery for almost all patients.

With late LB, there is disagreement about the best approach to treatment. The vast majority of medical practitioners would give a short course of antibiotics.[18] As with early LB, oral antibiotics are first used and parenteral antibiotics for 3 weeks if symptoms are severe. **For the vast majority of patients, this is sufficient and there is recovery.** Often, the patient's symptoms may gradually improve with time without further antibiotic treatment. The reason for this is that the patient's symptoms are not due to active organisms (which can be killed by antibiotics), but are due to the body's immune system dealing with the infection.

2. Prolonged courses of antibiotics.
There are some medical practitioners and patient organisations which advocate prolonged courses of antibiotics sometimes over years or decades. The argument is that the infection is difficult to treat and that there are relapses with LB. As with PVFS, relapses may be due to patients not staying within their energy limits and therefore antibiotics are not indicated. **Prolonged courses of antibiotics can be dangerous** and evidence supporting such an approach is usually based on individual patients. Unless there can be general evidence of such an approach, it is unlikely that most doctors would be happy in making such management

decisions.

3. Relapses or re-infections.

It is important to separate relapses from second infections. Obviously, **if a patient is being infected a second time (especially with a different strain of the organism), antibiotic treatment is indicated.** An important indication that this is a re-infection is that symptoms are severe and very much like the original infection (fever, headaches, rashes). However with relapses there tends to be more chronic symptoms such as fatigue, muscle pain and nerve dysfunction. A short course of antibiotics is indicated for re-infections.

4. Energy management.

As with PVFS, patients with late LB benefit from energy management. **The steps to recovery advocated in this book have produced great benefit in many patients** with late LB. It can be difficult for patients to think of a recovery programme lasting many months when they feel that a short course of antibiotics may produce recovery. Nevertheless, many of these patients end up taking prolonged courses of antibiotics over a timescale that is greater than the management programme in this book.

PRECAUTIONS

The best way to avoid getting LB is to avoid tick bites. If you are going into the countryside it is essential that you take adequate precautions[17].

1. Clothing.

Light clothing allows you to see ticks on your clothing more easily. It is also important that you have the

186

minimal amount of bared areas of skin. You should wear boots not sandals, trousers should be tucked into socks and long-sleeved shirts should be worn.

2. Tick Repellents.
There are several on the market but they are not as useful as making sure that your body is properly covered. Experienced walkers use tick repellents and take care to clothe themselves properly.

3. Body inspection.
The best way to avoid LB is to inspect your body after your activities. Often, ticks are able to get past your body defences even though you might be taking precautions. All ticks should be removed as quickly as possible. If the tick is removed within 24 hours, there is little chance of LB[17].

SUMMARY

1. There is a lot of misinformation on LB. Patients should get the correct facts.

2. There are private unaccredited laboratories offering tests for LB. These tests are unreliable.

3. Tests for late LB are dependable. A negative test implies that there is no LB.

4. Prolonged courses of antibiotics are not recommended.

Important facts

Although tick bites are very common, LB is rare. This is because the majority of ticks do not have infection. Less than 5% of PVFS patients have LB.

CHAPTER SIXTEEN
MEDICAL KNOWLEDGE AND ASSESSMENT

Most mistakes are made in the management of patients. There are many reasons for this: patients have complex problems; management takes time; results are not easy to evaluate; and there is controversy over the best treatment. **Thus PVFS patients are often given conflicting and wrong advice. What should the patient do?** Patients should approach their illness as stated in this book. Their doctor should be aware of their illness, its natural history and the value of supportive treatment. **Problems can arise when patients have unreasonable expectations of the medical profession.** In the last decade, medical management of PVFS has dramatically changed. These changes mean that there are now acceptable models of patient management. Management will be considered as follows: medical knowledge, assessment, treatment and the patient's role. The first two factors will be covered in this chapter and the last two in the next chapter.

MEDICAL KNOWLEDGE

Despite advances in medical knowledge of PVFS, it is still in its infancy. This is not because the syndrome is new. Indeed, there are extensive descriptions of the disorder, probably at least as early as the seventeenth century (Chapter Three). However, it is only recently that there has been a greater understanding and acceptance of PVFS. This change has been due to a combination of medical education and social circumstances. **In the past, medical students were taught that recovery from viral illnesses always occurs within weeks.** If the patient did not recover, it was because of "low moral fibre" or even "malingering". As with many other dogmas, this was wrong. PVFS is one of many exceptions to quick recovery from viral illness.

Social circumstances have also changed in the last decade. **In particular, individuals have much greater expectation of the medical profession and society spends more time and effort on being well.** These latter two factors have combined to motivate patients with PVFS to keep seeing their doctor. Much of the recent research into PVFS has been prompted by patients insisting that they are ill, and eventually well-motivated doctors finding evidence to support patients' claims. In some cases, the doctors themselves have been ill and faced with scepticism, they have instigated their own research. **Thus, a combination of factors has contrived to increase research and interest in PVFS.** In retrospect, it is not surprising that an illness which produces such morbidity should eventually force itself to the attention of the medical profession. The National Institute for Health and Clinical Excellence (NICE) has published guidelines for PVFS and these should be a considerable help[20].

Current medical knowledge allows some definite statements to be made about PVFS. The most important is that the disease exists. To most sufferers, this may appear to be an obvious statement. Yet, until recently many medical practitioners did not accept the existence of the illness. For medical progress to be made, the first major step is the general acceptance of the disease entity. Only then can there be widespread cooperation, observation, research and funding into the condition. This stage has been reached and now there is every likelihood of major breakthroughs in our understanding of PVFS.

A critical question is what causes the disease. The answer to this question is not easy and there is likely to be a number of factors. At the moment, it appears that the most important mechanism is immunological. The attempt by the body to deal with the initial infection results in serious damage to the immune system. Cells and organs throughout the body are caught up in the process. **It is comparable to a civil war in which innocent bystanders become involved,** and the effects of the war influence subsequent generations. Thus, in some patients there is widespread damage to the body during the initial assault, and this damage takes years to repair. In other patients, there may not be such widespread damage, but instead the immune system is severely affected. This is comparable to the state of an army after a major war. It is unable to effectively deal with other aggressors. **For these patients, the major problem is dealing with subsequent infection** which may not only last longer, but also deplete the available resources further.

What does this information mean for the patient and the doctor? To continue my analogy of a war further, the implication is that the body slowly recovers. However, in a very small number of patients, the onslaught may have been too much, and after a variable period of maladjustment, a more serious illness may develop. Such casualties are rare. For the majority there has to be a slow adjustment to changed circumstances. If one is injured, **there is little value in spending too much time asking why one became injured.** A more productive position is one that recognises the injury and adopts a lifestyle to deal with the new circumstances.

I am advocating a pragmatic approach. The body has been dealt a potentially mortal blow. It makes sense to change one's lifestyle so that the demands are reduced, thereby allowing the body to recover. In the future, there will be methods that will allow manipulation of the immune system. However, many treatments now available are unpredictable: some patients get better, some get worse and many remain the same. Three methods deserve particular mention: cognitive behaviour therapy, graded exercise and pacing. **I shall emphasise how these methods differ from my approach.**

1. Cognitive Behaviour Therapy (CBT)
In 1989, a model for PVFS was proposed in which the authors suggested that patients by avoiding exercise perpetuated their illness, and the answer was appropriate CBT[19]. My article in response to this paper showed that their model was applicable to only the long-term ill

patient. The recently-ill patient often tried to exercise to fitness, and it was the inability to recover which made the long-term ill reduce their exercise[7]. Subsequently, other workers have claimed that CBT aided recovery by **reducing** patients' belief that their illness was mainly physical, caused by a virus and exercise should be avoided. My response to this work was that I achieved similar benefits by **increasing** patients' belief in these areas[21]. So, what is the explanation of these apparent opposite points of view?

The best of CBT is when there is a collaborative rather than an adversarial approach between doctor and patient: problems are solved; there is education of the patient; sessions are structured; and treatment is time-limited. **Therefore, my approach to management uses the best of CBT.** A major difference between my management and those of others is that they insist on "graded exercise", whereas **I do not recommend increasing exercise until diary scores are 8/10.** This allows for an adverse reaction to activity, and the ability to get better.

2. Graded Exercise

This usually means a gradual increase in exercise. To the public, there is a vision of someone in a jogging suit running for many hours. However, to those who suggest graded exercise, it may mean someone who was previously in bed all day getting up and walking across the room. In some studies, supervised "graded exercise" is 5-15 mins per week for 12 weeks. My approach is that patients have a limited amount of energy (money), and **they must decide how to spend it.** If some want to walk or run, it is up to them, however **they must remain**

within their energy limits. My approach changes when patients are able to score 8/10 for at least 4-6 weeks. Then, **exercise is gradually increased.**

3. Pacing

This is a regime that involves activity and regular rest periods. The individual should feel rested from one activity before starting another. Some patients find this approach useful. Nevertheless, **there are several differences from my approach.** Many patients are in a state where they never feel rested. Also, with pacing the patient only stays within their energy levels; with my approach, I ask patients to save more energy on good days. However, overall, there are many similarities between the systems, and pacing is an off-shoot of my system. **My approach was documented a decade before pacing.**

MEDICAL ASSESSMENT

Better recovery from PVFS depends on a partnership between the doctor and patient. Like the best partnerships, this will require commitment and responsibility from both. Equally, it should be realised that **both are bringing different gifts to the partnership.** The doctor's role is in medical diagnosis and managing treatment. With PVFS patients, it can be more complicated and time-consuming and these are highlighted in the NICE guidelines. There are three objectives: to make a diagnosis, be aware of other diagnoses and to identify a patient's problems.

1. Diagnosis

The diagnosis of PVFS has been discussed in Chapter Five. **It is a clinical diagnosis and there are no definitive laboratory tests.** It is also what is called a "diagnosis of exclusion" (ie other conditions which may produce similar symptoms have to be excluded), and so the diagnosis must be made by a doctor. **In the vast majority of patients, there is no evidence of a continuing viral infection.** In a small number, there is evidence such as IgM antibodies (especially to Coxsackie or Epstein-Barr viruses), or raised IgG antibody titres. It is rare to grow the causative virus in samples from the patient. Other presumptive evidence that may be found in PVFS are low IgA levels, circulating immune complexes, changes in T (helper), T (suppressor) and natural killer cells[22]. **It must be emphasised that completely normal laboratory results are very common in patients with PVFS.** Although abnormal results can be comforting, they are **not** necessary to make the diagnosis.

Many patients are dismayed at the time taken for doctors to make the diagnosis. This delay is normal when the diagnosis is one of exclusion. In the past, in one study, the diagnosis was made only when 92% of patients were ill for more than one year, and 39% were ill for more than 11 years[23]. **Matters then improved and the majority of patients were diagnosed within 6 months (Figure 27).** My impression now is that 80% receive a diagnosis within 6 months, but 5% may be ill for more that one year. **Some doctors still have great difficulty in accepting PVFS as the diagnosis.** This may be because the patient's history is particularly complicated, and especially if there are emotional

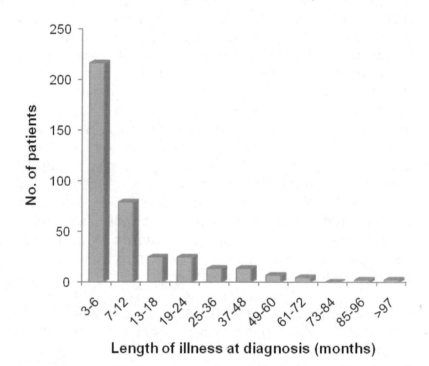

Figure 27   Length of illness at diagnosis
In a detailed study, the majority of patients (56%) were
diagnosed when they were ill for 3-6 months, and only 9%
were ill for more than 2 years[1].

problems. Other patients may have obvious psychiatric illness. **It is good practice for a doctor to take time in making a diagnosis.** In some cases, I have said to patients that I am unclear as to the precise diagnosis, but **that in the next 3-4 months, the diagnosis should become obvious.**

A strong point in favour of the diagnosis is **the typical history of a previously healthy, athletic individual** who has delayed recovery from a viral illness. An attempt should be made to establish if there is continuing infection by taking appropriate blood and other samples. **In most cases the results will be negative,** but they are also useful in establishing a baseline in a group of patients with many problems. Immunological studies, especially assessing T (helper), T (suppressor) and natural killer cells, may help the diagnosis.

Doctors should also attempt **to identify if there is one protracted illness or several illnesses.** I am frequently faced with patients who insist that they have been ill for "over ten years" or even "all my life" and "since I was a child". However, on detailed questioning, it usually becomes obvious that patients behaved normally for much of their lives. Usually **it is possible to identify the start of the illness when tiredness was greater than 50% of normal.** The next problem is to determine if there were periods of 6-8 weeks of normality during the years of illness. In most patients, there is not one continuing illness, but two or three attacks of illness. **This is important as patients with second or third attacks do better than patients with a continuing illness.** This is simply because if one can recover once, it is possible to do it again.   It is a very good sign for patients and the doctor.

2. Differential diagnosis
In medicine, a differential diagnosis is when you consider the possible causes of a patient's complaints.   In addition, PVFS is diagnosed by excluding other causes of the patient's complaints.   There are several conditions which are frequently confused with PVFS, and which need to be managed differently.

a) Chronic Pain Syndrome: In this condition, pain of muscles and/or joints is the principal complaint.   Patients would often say that they did not mind the tiredness, but the pain was intolerable.   Although there is muscle or joint pain in about a third of PVFS patients, the **tiredness is always greater than the pain.**   In patients with Chronic Pain Syndrome, the pain may seriously disturb sleep.   As with PVFS, reduced sleep makes tiredness worse.   Patients should be given pain killers and sleeping tablets to try and improve sleep.   Management of Chronic Pain Syndrome is different from PVFS.   Patients are reassured that their pain is not serious, and encouraged to tolerate the pain.   **Therefore the pain remains the same but the effect of the pain on the patient is much less.**   In contrast with PVFS, the tiredness (and pain) improves with management.   Patients should use the daily diary to record scores for pain and tiredness, and emphasise hours of sleep.

b) Primary Fibromyalgia Syndrome: In this condition, there are characteristic tender points in the body (Figure 28).   In PVFS, it is usually tender muscle groups that are found,   especially   muscles   of   the   limbs.   In   Primary

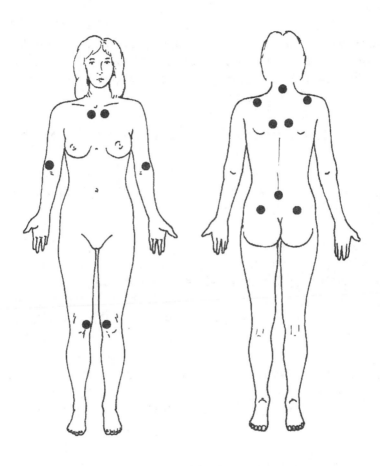

Figure 28   Primary Fibromyalgia Syndrome
There are tender points at 14 characteristic sites in Primary
Fibromyalgia Syndrome[24].

Fibromyalgia Syndrome, there are tender points over bony areas which does not happen in PVFS. Patients also have a different epidemiology, and I found a 99:1 ratio of PVFS to Primary Fibromyalgia Syndrome[24]. **The management of Primary Fibromyalgia Syndrome is to control sleep and increase activities.** This is one condition which benefits from increasing exercise at an early stage of the illness.

c) Psychiatric illness: This is discussed in Chapter Six.

d) Other associated conditions: These are less important, but the usual associated conditions are discussed in Chapter Six.

3. Identify the Patient's Problems
As with most individuals accustomed to good health, **PVFS patients do not adjust well to being ill.** Their complaints are many. Their anger and frustration with the medical profession and their situation is intense. Much time has to be spent in penetrating this barrier of anger and frustration. Although in all patients the principal complaint is tiredness, in some patients other complaints can be very worrying. Many patients have severe headaches and others can complain of incapacitating dizziness. These complaints have to be treated symptomatically; however, if PVFS is the cause of the complaint, **there is always improvement as the diary scores get better.**

It is essential that there is a good relationship between the doctor and the patient[20]. Both need to be able to trust each other. **Where such trust exists, it is easier for the doctor to identify the patient's problems,** ascertain the most likely cause and prescribe the most appropriate treatment. The important decision as to whether a symptom is due to PVFS, or to something else is for the doctor to make. The doctor will also need to establish if there are other problems, in particular those related to work, finances and relationships. **If these other problems are not resolved, recovery will be delayed.**

SUMMARY

1. Doctors accept the existence of PVFS, but much more research is needed.

2. My interpretation of cognitive behaviour therapy is in the management programme described in this book. Graded exercise can be harmful as exercise should increase only when diary scores are 8/10. Pacing has limitations.

3. Medical assessment is important to distinguish Chronic Pain Syndrome, Primary Fibromyalgia Syndrome, psychiatric illness and other associated conditions as these require different management.

Important facts

Management of PVFS patients is not easy. There are many theories on how to manage patients. It is best to have definite criteria for diagnosis and differentiate PVFS from other conditions. A good relationship between doctor and patient produces the best results.

CHAPTER SEVENTEEN

TREATMENT

This chapter deals with supportive and drug treatments and the patients' role in treatment. It should be read in conjunction with Chapter 16.

SUPPORTIVE TREATMENT

In PVFS, treatment is mainly supportive. The word "supportive" in this context is used to mean treatment that can be given to patients to alleviate their symptoms. Doctors should encourage patients to help themselves, support the patient and understand self-help groups.

1. Encourage Patients to Help Themselves

Initially, patients spend a lot of time talking about their illness to anyone who is prepared to listen. The patients expect the medical profession to produce a dramatic cure. **After months or years, many patients stop talking about the illness and turn to fringe medicine for a cure.** This progression in the patient's behaviour and attitude is a reflection of the limitations of medical treatment. Often, too, doctors may not be aware that the patient's confidence in them is at a low level. The answer is to encourage patients to help themselves. **The change from finding one's own solutions to problems, rather than expecting someone else to do so is a major one.** It is the start of better recovery. The approach that is advocated is for the doctor to allow patients to adopt the five steps to recovery (Figure 29).

2. Support the patient
Perhaps more than anything else, **the patient appreciates the doctor's support.** Common complaints are: "My doctor does not believe that I am ill" or "Why does my doctor want me to see a psychiatrist?" These two examples are probably breakdowns in communication rather than lack of support from the doctor. Nevertheless, they highlight the fact that PVFS patients require a lot of the doctor's time. This is not surprising. **All patients with chronic illness, especially those who are young, need to have their illness explained to them.** Support should have two main objectives. First, the patient's mental state is particularly vulnerable and much time needs to be spent in reassurance. Secondly, patients require symptomatic treatment for many complaints. It is in this area that the relationship between doctor and patient is tested. In addition, many patients require advice on Alternative Medicine (Chapter Fourteen).

3. Self-help groups
Doctors must understand self-help groups. As with all such organisations, doctors have to be aware of the objects of the group and I have written a chapter on this subject in the 3rd edition of this book. Although some may do harm, the national organisations can be

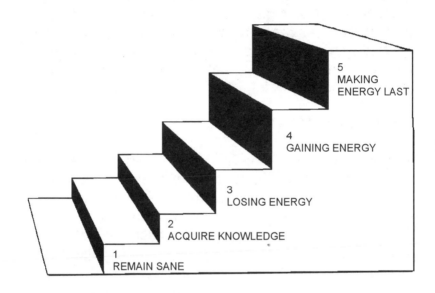

Figure 29   Steps to recovery

There are five main steps to recovery and each step is of varying height, representing its difficulty. The whole objective is to understand energy. Each step is further explained in separate chapters in this book.

recommended (ME Association, Action for ME). The NICE guidelines[20] recognise that self-help groups may help. In my experience, **patients have derived great benefit from being a member of a national self-help group**[25]. I am very impressed by **Ellen Piro** who founded the Norwegian ME Association in 1986. Her organisation has made significant progress in raising ME matters with politicians and also providing a good service for the members. Also, local groups such as the Bristol group can be very helpful, focussed, and vibrant.

DRUG TREATMENT

The medical profession is accustomed to prescribing drugs and many patients come to expect being given a tablet to cure their ills. The problem in PVFS is that the **effect of drugs can be less predictable.** Thus, a drug may do harm and make a patient feel like a "zombie". Yet, these drugs in other patients may relieve their symptoms and give them a good night's sleep. It is the doctor's responsibility to find drugs that work. And the patient must understand that several drugs may have to be tried before the useful one is found. Drug treatment, its success and the problems are as follows:

Treatment	Success	Problems
1. Pain killers	Good	Few
2. Antidepressants	Good	Several
3. Sleeping tablets	Very good	Several
4. Anti-fungal measures	Fair	Many
5. Vitamins and minerals	Poor	Many
6. Other drugs	Poor	Great

As with alternative medicine, some medical practitioners are reluctant to prescribe any of the therapies in the list. The difficulty is that these therapies can have significant disadvantages. Equally, patients can be reluctant to accept medical help. My position is that the medical profession can offer limited help to PVFS patients, **but if the conditions are right such help can be valuable aids.**

1. Pain Killers
If patients moderate their activity, pain is reduced. Pain is also a useful sign; it tells patients that they are doing too much. Patients with muscle pain find it easier to control their activities than patients without muscle pain. A significant number of patients may go on to develop muscle pain. I believe that patients should first try to moderate their activities and understand energy. Nevertheless, I recognise that some patients may be helped by medication. I would initially use **paracetamol.** This is the initial drug of choice. In about a quarter of patients, **pain disturbs sleep and more potent pain-killers may be required for a short time.** Dihydrocodeine (DF-118) can be useful. The non-steroidal anti-inflammatory group of drugs can help. Ibuprofen is probably the most helpful and diclofenac (Voltarol) is worth trying. **For each patient, it is worth trying several pain killers as persistence is frequently rewarded.**

2. Antidepressants
My initial management of patients with mild depression is in Chapter Six. **About a quarter of PVFS patients require antidepressants at some time.** Tricyclic antidepressants can make patients feel like a "zombie",

but very small doses of these medications may improve symptoms. The dosage should start at the lowest possible and gradually increase until the patient feels better but does not have a hangover. **There are several groups of antidepressants drugs with different usefulness and side-effects.** These drugs take time to act, usually 14-28 days; and conversely have to be withdrawn slowly. The many side-effects of antidepressants can be a limiting factor in their use. Some of these side-effects are common and some uncommon, but the doctor must be aware of all potential side-effects of each drug. Antidepressants also interact with many other drugs that a patient may be taking. Usually a doctor gets to know a few drugs in each group of antidepressants. Thus, if there are problems with one drug, another can be tried. It is important that **the patient accepts that finding the right drug may take some time.** The choice of drugs is usually made from the following:

a)   tricyclic antidepressants with sedative effects such as **amitriptyline** or **dosulepin**.

b)   tricyclic antidepressants that are less sedative such as **imipramine** or **lofepramine**.

c)   selective serotonin re-uptake inhibitors with fewer side-effects, such as **sertraline** (lustral) or **paroxetine** (seroxat).

d)   other antidepressants that are for severe depressive illness or more specialist use.

For PVFS patients, the topic of antidepressants can be very emotive. Patients resist taking antidepressants because of their stigma. **However, tricyclic antidepressants at low dose are good at improving sleep.** Also if you are getting better on antidepressants, you must not suddenly stop taking them. The daily dose needs to be reduced very gradually. Depression can lead to suicide and must be taken seriously. Doctors are happier to prescribe some antidepressants rather than sleeping tablets as the former are designed for long term use.

3. Sleeping Tablets
My first approach to patients with sleeping problems is to get them to understand energy. Many patients can be too tired or anxious to sleep and **moderating activity can result in better sleep. At the same time, I recommend unwind exercises.** These may be combined with the traditional remedies of **honey in warm milk, hot drinking chocolate at night or a short massage.** Some patients can also benefit from a long, hot bath; however, other patients may be made considerably worse by a hot bath. If after two months, there is no improvement, sleeping tablets should be considered.

The problem with sleeping tablets is that the patient may become dependent on them, and long term use produces tolerance (the tablets do not have the same effects). Thus, the best approach is to use these tablets for short periods, such as 1-3 weeks. **A 3-week course may break a bad sleeping cycle,** even though some patients may feel worse whilst on treatment, they are often better when treatment stops. Generally, the doctor should try several preparations and it is usually possible to find one which benefits the patient. The reluctance of some doctors to prescribe sleeping tablets has resulted in some patients using tablets that can be bought over-the-counter. The most frequently used are anti-histamines that have a sedative effect. Good examples are **diphenhydramine** and **promethazine**. These drugs should not be used more than 3 weeks tolerance may develop.

The most common group of prescription drugs are the benzodiazepines. The short acting benzodiazepines last for 12-18 hours but in PVFS patients can continue to act the next day (eg. **temazepam**, **lormetazepam**). The medium acting benzodiazepines have effects the next day and are best avoided (eg. nitrazepam). There is no doubt that PVFS patients are more sensitive to these drugs and the effects may be prolonged. It is important that low doses are first tried with these drugs. Non-benzodiazepine hypnotics are available and are better for short-term use. They appear to give a good quality sleep and are again best used initially in half doses. Good examples of these are **zopiclone, zaleplon** and **zolpidem.** All these drugs are not designed for long term use and some patients have developed dependence.

4. Anti-Fungal Measures

The suggestion that fungal infections such as yeast infection (especially *Candida albicans*) may cause or aggravate PVFS has been discussed for decades. Those who are good candidates for yeast infection are women, especially if they are on the contraceptive pill or on an immunosuppressant. In such patients, because of the difficulty in diagnosing low-grade fungal infection, a short course of an anti-fungal drug **(eg nystatin or fluconazole)** may be tried. **A few patients have had considerable benefit, but most are unaffected.** Some practitioners have advocated large doses of nystatin combined with an anti-Candida diet. There are various claims for the success of this approach, but in my experience only a few patients benefit. Diets can be very time consuming and expensive (Chapter Eleven), and often the patient has to still recover from PVFS. **It is likely that candida (or other yeasts) infection may make PVFS worse, but that such infection is not the cause of PVFS.** Nevertheless, some patients, especially those with long-lasting illness may have improvement of their abdominal complaints with an anti-Candida diet.

5. Vitamins and Minerals
Extra vitamins, especially large doses of Vitamin C, B6 and B12 have been used in PVFS patients. My feelings about extra vitamins (Chapter Eleven) are that **they are unnecessary in an individual who is eating normally.** It has also been suggested that extra minerals may be of benefit. In particular, weekly injections of **magnesium** have been advocated. Low red blood cell magnesium may result from many other conditions such as inactivity (which can be common in PVFS patients) or hypothyroidism. The role of magnesium in PVFS is unproven and most other workers have not confirmed the initial results. It is probably not wise to give magnesium to patients unless they have low red blood cell magnesium and have normal kidney function.

Zinc is an essential mineral for good health. It also has anti-viral effects and is important in immune function, but is present in many foods and supplements are usually not necessary. Similarly, it has been suggested that **selenium** may moderate the individual's immune response to viral infections. However, there is no good evidence that selenium supplements may benefit PVFS patients.

6. Other drugs

Every fortnight **there is a new suggested measure that may benefit PVFS patients.** Suggestions may be totally anecdotal, such as bee stings or electric shocks. Alternatively, they may have some scientific basis. For example, **Coenzyme Q10** has been advocated. This enzyme is present in mitochondria (which are the batteries of human cells) and plays an important role in energy production. This substance may also neutralise harmful toxins, but there are no studies showing benefit of this enzyme to many PVFS patients.

Unlike the position with bacterial infections, specific treatment with **anti-viral agents** is developing. Thus, there are anti-viral agents against some herpes viruses which are very effective such as **acyclovir (zovirax) and ganciclovir (cymevene).** Many drugs have also been developed to act against human immunodeficiency virus, hepatitis B, hepatitis C and influenza viruses. None of these agents have been shown to have proven benefits for PVFS patients. In the future, anti-viral agents may have a role in specific treatment. There are considerable risks to patients in adopting unproven remedies. **Many patients have been made considerably worse, and many have been made financially bankrupt.** I believe that it is better for patients to understand energy rather than try for instant cures.

PATIENT'S ROLE

When patients are told that they have a major role to play in managing their illness, there is usually disbelief. **They cannot believe that they have to adopt the five steps to better recovery.** Many patients react with "But what about the doctors? After all, it's their job to make me better". Although this is essentially true, in PVFS there is no effective treatment currently available. Management depends upon maintaining the patient's confidence, and attempting to alleviate any symptoms that are present. **The traditional medical approach of treatment with drugs and tablets is doomed to failure.** Recovery is best achieved by patients changing their lifestyle to take into account their body's changed capabilities. The doctor's role is secondary – not to treat PVFS, but to ensure that the patient does not have any other treatable illness. When new symptoms develop, doctors are able to provide reassurance that there is no other cause of the symptoms. **When patients know that they have PVFS, they can start to understand their symptoms and modify their behaviour accordingly.** The role of patients is to understand the media; take responsibility for their illness; and find their own answers.

1. The Media

Many patients are very influenced by adverse reports in the media. Such articles and programmes are often interpreted as direct criticism by the patient. This emotional reaction is very difficult to deal with and may even cause a relapse. This is sad and unnecessary. **Patients should recognise that the media frequently gets its facts wrong.** When patients see or hear adverse comments, they should not react with anger, horror or disgust. Instead, they should ask the simple question: "Are the facts correct?" If the answer is no, the programme or article should be ignored. If the answer is yes, patients should think again about why their reactions were negative. Often, patients feel that a personal attack has been made on their credibility. **This is an over-reaction.**

Many doctors are greatly annoyed at having to deal with upset patients after media attention. It will be a great relief to doctors if patients are able to see these news stories in perspective. One does not go to see one's Member of Parliament after every political story in the media. In the vast majority of cases, the relevance of a political story to the patient's life is the same as a PVFS story. However, **with the hurt of illness, it is easy to get media stories out of perspective.**

2. Personal Responsibility
Many patients treat **PVFS like a bit of sticky tape which they keep trying to throw away.** They fail and the tape keeps getting stuck to their clothing and shoes, causing great annoyance. **In fact PVFS is a giant cross which has to be carried.** It is a full time job, requiring all of the patient's resources. It cannot and should not be forgotten that if one is carrying a heavy load, loss of concentration results in a stumble, then a fall. **The medical management of PVFS requires that patients take responsibility for their illness.** Patients derive greatest help from themselves (Figure 30). Patients need to adopt a plan and undertake the steps to recovery

HELP IN PVFS

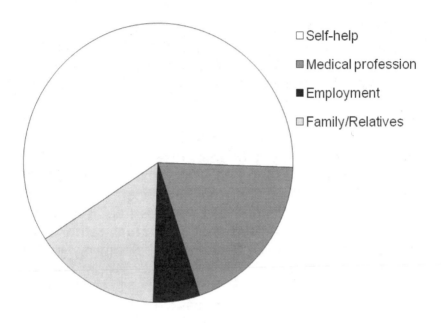

☐ Self-help

■ Medical profession

■ Employment

☐ Family/Relatives

Figure 30   Help in PVFS
Patients obtain greatest help from themselves.   Their close
family or relatives are next most important.   Supportive help
provided by the medical profession, and an understanding
employer can also be a great asset.

(Figure 29). It will not be easy. In most cases it will be the most difficult task that they have ever undertaken. **As with many difficulties in life, survival and good health can be great prizes.**

3. Finding Answers

As every parent knows, children find it easy to ask questions. However, part of the upbringing of children is to teach the children to find answers to their own questions. Similarly, PVFS patients need to find their own answers to their questions. Before one is able to find answers to problems, **it is necessary to have an accurate assessment of the current position.** Most patients would describe their current position as: "a disaster", "chaos", or "grief and mega-grief". Whilst these expressions are colourful, and perhaps true, **it is better to have an assessment that is factual rather than emotional.** Therefore: "I cannot cope with my job" is more useful than: "My life is a disaster". Simply, one can devise a strategy to cope with facts, but to deal with an emotional problem may be impossible.

Patients must know how they have spent every hour of the day. **Every day is not the same.** Many, many times patients have refused to do their daily diary because they felt that "every day was the same". As an example, I am frequently told that "I rested all day", or "All I do is rest". In many of these cases, the diary scores showed no improvement. To deal with this problem, I decided that **the word "rest" hid too many activities.** Instead, I found that patients in this situation often were resting physically but were very active mentally. They were losing energy mentally and spending more than they had. This is why I prefer "unwind" as this means that there is mental and physical reduction in activities. I like to hear patients say: **"I unwind most of the day"**.

SUMMARY

1. Supportive medical treatment requires the doctor to encourage patients to help themselves, and self-help groups may be of great benefit.

2. Drug treatment can be complicated as the doctor attempts to find the correct pain killer, antidepressant or sleeping tablet.

3. In the short term, sleeping tablets can be of great help in breaking a bad sleep cycle.

4. Other drug treatments are at an early stage of development and may benefit only a few patients.

5. The patient's role in management involves an understanding of the media, taking personal responsibility for the illness and finding his/her own answers to questions.

Important facts

The most important treatment is for the patient to understand energy as this can help all symptoms. For short periods, doctors can offer drug treatments. It may take some time before the right drugs are found. Matters will be helped if both patient and doctor can show good humour during this difficult process.

CHAPTER EIGHTEEN
CONCLUSION

In the late eighties in London, young dealers in the city could make one million pounds for their company before lunch. They had two bottle lunches and only drank champagne. In the same place, Buddy lived. He was a teenager who had run away from home and lived on the streets. He was regarded as being very simple. The young dealers would pour out onto the pavement after their hundred pounds lunches and stop to speak to Buddy. Buddy amused them and made them feel good.

They would say: "Buddy! What would you choose between this shiny metal fifty pence coin and an old paper ten pound note?" Buddy would always hesitate, he would point a grubby finger at one and then the other. His eyes would widen and he would always choose the fifty pence coin. The young dealers would laugh and shake their heads in dismay at Buddy's predicament. Each day he would perform at least fifty times.

The terrible nineties came and most of the young dealers lost their jobs. One day, one dealer who had been unemployed for two years returned. He saw Buddy, felt remorse and said:

"Buddy, I have to tell you the ten pound paper note is worth more than the shiny metal fifty pence coin".

"Oh yes, I know! But if I choose the ten pound note, I would not get offered the choice again. Anyway, I'm still in work and you are looking for a job".

PVFS patients have to choose less to get more; like Buddy, it is the long-term results that are important. It is also a matter of pride − it is not easy to play the Buddy role. It is very hard to pretend that you are dumb when you are not; it is very difficult to have people laugh at you. But, who is more mature in this story? And who gains most? Many PVFS patients feel that their past was full of adventure and good times. Now, they have bad cards. They see their acquaintances, often with less ability (but more energy), doing well and apparently prospering. In comparison, a patient's lot seems to be coming to terms with constant fatigue, intermittent infections, unemployment, separation and divorce. **There seems to be only one major life-event to come − death; and, many wish it soon.**

Patients spend a lot of time mourning their past existence. They remember times when the sun always shone, when there was frenetic activity and applause. Their current lives appear to be rainy days, pain, discomfort and sadness. **Like all mourning, the whole exercise can take six months.** Sadly, patients are as in Figure 31. They gradually find themselves in the bog of PVFS. Fortunately, there is a path through the bog. **The path is difficult and there are many opportunities for disaster.** Yet, there is also much scope to get more out

220

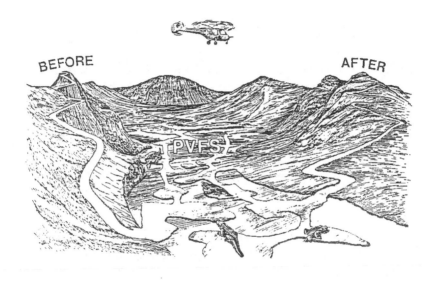

Figure 31   The bog of PVFS
Patients want the medical profession to take them, in a helicopter, from the mountain top before PVFS to the mountain top after PVFS.   This helicopter does not exist.   Instead, patients gradually slide into the bog of PVFS.   But there is a path through this bog.   The way to recovery is there but difficult to find.

of life. Anyone can do well when they have unlimited resources. **The real test of ability is to succeed with very limited resources.** PVFS patients have very, very limited resources.

FUTURE MEDICAL TREATMENT

With PVFS, one hypothesis is that **in a small number of people, during an acute viral infection, there is widespread immunological damage to many tissues.** The damage to these tissues may take years to be repaired. In addition, many patients have an immunological system that continues to function abnormally, and this can cause additional damage, thereby further delaying a return to good health. In the next few decades, it is likely that it will be possible to correct the immunological abnormalities that follow the acute infection. **Thus, the continuing damage to the body's tissues will be prevented,** and the principal effects of PVFS will be confined to injuries to tissues during the acute viral infection.

An even more profound effect on patients with PVFS is also possible. In the above hypothesis it is assumed that most of the damage is done at the time of the acute infection. This may be incorrect. Another suggestion is that **the continuing malfunction of the immune system is responsible for the continuing disease.** Thus, the disease can be cured if the immunological abnormalities are corrected. In time, the truth will be known, but whichever hypothesis is correct, medical manipulation of the immune system will be of great help to PVFS patients. **Future decades will also see developments in augmenting the body's ability to**

ADVANTAGES

Are there any advantages in the patient's situation? What are the "equalizers"? There are two. First is how the patient copes with PVFS. This is a university, an assault course, a test of survival; **graduation and survival will ingrain patients with a deep knowledge of themselves.** The second is in the patient's potential for happiness. Perhaps, the only equality in the world is each individual's potential for happiness. Each person, no matter how disadvantaged, probably has the same amount of potential for happiness each day as the most privileged. **Happiness is there, it is free; but, many refuse to take their allotted portion, simply because they are ill.** Illness can give patients the understanding that they can be happy if they choose to be – every day.

Life is short. For many, it is a catalogue of lost opportunities. **Patients have to decide if PVFS is a disaster or an opportunity.** The way to better recovery involves personal commitment, hard work, self-understanding and the need for optimism. Very few in the population are given the situation that requires acquisition of such qualities. One should remember that great pressures, over many years, are required to make a diamond – the hardest of all minerals, able to withstand much stress. **A PVFS patient has a terrible affliction at the wrong time of life.** Yet, coping with the illness and its consequences produces a very special person: **one capable of coping with strife, but able to enjoy the sunshine between the storms.**

REFERENCES

1. Ho-Yen DO. The epidemiology of Post Viral Fatigue Syndrome. Scot Med J 1988; 33: 368-9.

2. Bramwell E. Discussion on Encephalitis Lethargica. Br Med J 1921; ii: 648-52.

3. Bredeck JF, Brown GO, Hempelmann TC, McFadden JF, Spector HI. Follow-up studies of the 1933 St Louis epidemic of encephalitis. JAMA 1938; iii: 15-7.

4. Ho-Yen DO and McNamara I. General practitioners' experience of the chronic fatigue syndrome. Br J Gen Pract 1991; 41: 324-6.

5. Hickie I, Davenport T, Wakefield D et al. Post-infective and chronic fatigue syndromes precipitated by viral and non-viral pathogens: prospective cohort studies. Br Med J 2006; 333: 575-8.

6. Manu P, Lane TJ, Matthews DA. The frequency of the chronic fatigue syndrome in patients with symptoms of persistent fatigue. An Intern Med 1988; 109: 554-6.

7. Ho-Yen DO. Patient management of Post Viral Fatigue Syndrome. Br J Gen Pract 1990; 40: 37-9.

8. Shanks MF and Ho-Yen DO. A Clinical Study of Chronic Fatigue Syndrome. Br J Psych 1995; 166: 798-801.

9. Ho-Yen DO. Definitions for doubting GPs. Physician 1990; 581-3.

10. Lane RJH, Soteriou BA, Zhang H, Archard LC. Enterovirus related metabolic myopathy: a postviral fatigue syndrome. J Neurol Neurosurg Psychiatry 2003; 74: 1382-6.

11. Jammes Y, Steinberg JG, Mambrini O et al. Chronic fatigue syndrome: assessment of increased oxidative stress and altered muscle excitability in response to incremental exercise. J Int Med 2005; 257: 299-310.

12. Hooper M. Myalgic encephalomyelitis: a review with emphasise on key findings in biomedical research. J Clin Pathol 2007; 60: 466-71.

13. Pearson DJ. Pseudo food allergy. Br Med J 1986; 292: 221-2.

14. Smith R. Without work all life goes rotten. Br Med J 1992; 305: 972.

15. Colby J. ME: The new plague. First and Best in Education. 1996: Ipswich.

16. Loudon I. A brief history of homeopathy. J Roy Soc Med 2006; 99: 607-10.

17. Blackwell A, Hendry G, Ho-Yen DO. Ticks, your pets, your family and you. 2006 Mercat Press: Edinburgh.

18. Wormser GP, Dattwyler RJ, Shapiro ED et al. The clinical assessment, treatment and prevention of Lyme Disease, Human Granulocytic Anaplasmosis and Babesiosis: clinical practice guidelines by the Infectious Diseases Society of America. Clin Infect Dis 2006; 43: 1089-134.

19. Wessely S, David A, Butter S, Chalder T. Management of chronic (post viral) fatigue syndrome. Br J Gen Pract 1989; 39: 26-9.

20. Baker R, Shaw EJ et al. Diagnosis and management of chronic fatigue syndrome or myalgic encephalomyelitis (encephalopathy): summary of NICE guidance. BrMed J 2007; 335: 446-8.

21. Ho-Yen DO. Patients' beliefs about their illness were probably not a major factor. Br Med J 1996; 312: 1097-8.

22. Ho-Yen DO, Billington RW, Urquhart J. Natural Killer Cells and Post Viral Fatigue Syndrome. Scand J Infect Dis 1991; 23: 711-16.

23. Wookey C. Myalgic Encephalomyelitis. Post Viral Fatigue Syndrome and how to cope with it. 1986 Croom Helm: London.

24. Ho-Yen DO. Chronic Fatigue Syndrome and Fibromyalgia. Br Med J 1994; 309: 1515.

25. Ho-Yen DO and Grant A. Self-help groups give valuable support. Br Med J 1994; 308: 1298-9.

APPENDIX: HOW TO USE THIS BOOK

Many readers have asked me how to use this book. The type and fonts have been designed to be read by those with poor memories. However, the book is also not designed to read from page 1.

A. START
- Read Chapter 1.
- Read important facts of Chapters 2-5.
- Read Chapters 6-9.
- Implement Chapters 6-9.

B. INDIVIDUAL PROBLEMS
- Read Chapter dealing with problem, e.g. employment.
- Read Chapters 6-9.

C. RELAPSE
- Try to identify a cause of the relapse.
- Read Summaries of Chapters 6-9.
- Ask yourself if you are doing what is stated in Chapters 6-9.

D. GREATER KNOWLEDGE
- Read Important Facts of each chapter.
- If interested, read Summaries of each chapter.
- If still interested, read the chapter.

E. REVISION

- Keep re-reading Chapters 6-9.
- Keep re-reading Important Facts.
- Read other chapters and summaries only when you are getting better.

F. USEFUL TIPS

- Highlight important sentences in the book with a highlighter pen and put "Post-it" markers so that you can refer back to these passages.
- Make a note of sections of the book that you think do not refer to you. Often patients make this assumption because what is being asked is too difficult and would require a change in lifestyle.
- Repetition in the book is annoying when you are getting better. When you are ill, you do not notice the repetition.

INDEX

A Scientist's Quest for God in daily life.

(ISBN 0-951109-06-5)

by Dr Darrel Ho-Yen

As he approaches 50 years of age, the author is forced to question his religious beliefs.

His 30 years of medical research experience should have been an asset in his quest to live his religious beliefs, but answers do not come easily.

Seven years later after reading some 60 books and the Bible twice, a plan is developed. Many will not find the answers acceptable, however, the results represent a lot of work and study.

Some of the observations may be helpful. The plan has been tried and tested and may be particularly useful to those who are housebound.

Obtainable from: **Dodona Books (www.dodonabooks.co.uk)**

Unwind!

Understand and control life, be better!

(ISBN 0-9511090-2-2)

by Dr Darrel Ho-Yen

Many individuals are having great difficulties in living in a modern society. This stress may produce ill health. This book shows that stress can be reduced by the acquisition of skills. **This book was first published in 1991 and reprinted in 1994 and many patients still find it valuable.**

The skill of unwinding (EMBME) is explained in great detail and has benefits of physical and mental relaxation. **Both well and ill individuals would benefit from this skill.**

With the ability to unwind, you can start to develop an understanding of your life and identify your own problems. Control of your life is achieved by good use of time, use of the reward/effort ratio and good decision-making. **With the acquisition of these skills, you have the opportunity for self-improvement, happiness and to be better.**

Obtainable from: **Dodona Books (www.dodonabooks.co.uk)**

Climbing Out of The Pit of Life

(ISBN 0-9511090-4-9)

by Dr Darrel Ho-Yen

The pit of life may be many things: death of a loved one, the end of a relationship, severe illness, financial ruin, a severe accident, betrayal, public humiliation, loss of a job or an enforced change of life.

How do some people recover quickly whilst others may never recover? How does one cope with these crises? The ladder (**l**ifeless, **a**nger, **d**enial, **d**isgrace, **e**ndeavour, **r**enewal) describes the stages one needs to go through to cope with great loss.

The symptoms of each stage are described and detailed information is provided on how to progress to the next stage. **With this knowledge, quick recovery is possible.** Since its publication in 1995, many have been helped.

Obtainable from: **Dodona Books (www.dodonabooks.co.uk)**